Creating an
Economic Development
Action Plan

Creating an Economic Development Action Plan

A Guide for Development Professionals
Revised and Updated Edition

THOMAS S. LYONS
and
ROGER E. HAMLIN

Westport, Connecticut
London

Library of Congress Cataloging-in-Publication Data

Lyons, Thomas S.
    Creating an economic development action plan : a guide for development
professionals / Thomas S. Lyons and Roger E. Hamlin.—Rev. and updated ed.
        p.   cm.
    Includes bibliographical references and index.
    ISBN 0–275–96808–1 (alk. paper)—ISBN 0–275–96809–X (pbk. : alk. paper)
    1. Economic development—Planning.   2. Community development—Planning.   I.
Hamlin, Roger E.   II. Title.
    HD87.5.L96   2001
    338.9'0068'4—dc21   00–058010

British Library Cataloguing in Publication Data is available.

Library of Congress Catalog Card Number: 00–058010
ISBN: 0–275–96808–1
        0–275–96809–X (pbk.)

First published in 2001

Praeger Publishers, 88 Post Road West, Westport, CT 06881
An imprint of Greenwood Publishing Group, Inc.
www.praeger.com

Printed in the United States of America

The paper used in this book complies with the
Permanent Paper Standard issued by the National
Information Standards Organization (Z39.48–1984).

10 9 8 7 6 5 4 3 2

Contents

Tables and Figures

Acknowledgments

As with the first edition, this second edition is designed to apply the rational, systematic approach of the planning process to development of a local economy. The book's layout and content reflect this intention. We hope the reader will come away with a fuller understanding of the economic development planning process, a greater appreciation for the role of economic development in overall community development, and some ideas for formulating creative and effective economic development strategies.

In attempting to accomplish these objectives, we have drawn on the knowledge, expertise, and efforts of countless others, to whom we owe a debt of gratitude. Credit for many of the program ideas described in Chapter 4, for example, should be extended to the citizens of numerous communities with whom we have worked over the years. This fact is further testimony that a local planner's best resource is the citizenry itself. Versions of the example programs suggested in that chapter were generated by planning commissions and economic development committees, and tested by those communities over several years.

We would also like to acknowledge the many economic development professionals with whom we have had the opportunity to work. Their insights are reflected throughout this book. In particular, we would like to thank Dr. Gregg A. Lichtenstein for his leading-edge thinking included in the sections on "Business Incubation Program" and "Social

Capital Building for Business Retention" in Chapter 4. In addition, we gratefully acknowledge Shelonda R. Stewart, Manager of Training and Technical Assistance for the Business Plus microenterprise program in Louisville, Kentucky, and Cheri Davis-Taylor, of the Enterprise Management Group, for their insights into micro-lending and microenterprise development. Regarding the Capital Access Program, we offer thanks to Karen Ammarman and Larry Schrauben of the Michigan Economic Development Corporation and Ben Jones and Clifford Kellogg of the U.S. Department of the Treasury. Notwithstanding all of the expertise and assistance provided us, any errors of fact are our own.

Our continued thanks to Carol Robards Croop for the original graphics used in several figures in this book and its first edition and to our editors at Praeger for their extensive publication expertise. Finally, we would like to express gratitude to our families for their unending patience and support during years of heavy travel schedules, lengthy research time, and difficult publication deadlines related to this and several previous books and publications.

Introduction

Despite strong economies in recent years in the United States and Canada, economic development remains an important and widely recognized local government activity. This is due, in part, to the persistent poverty that plagues some urban neighborhoods and communities and many rural towns. Also, local governments everywhere know economies are cyclical; no "boom" lasts forever. Another contributor to the importance of economic development is the continued existence of organizational infrastructure created in the 1980s and early 1990s. In response to periods of economic recession and their accompanying high unemployment, competition intensified between state, provincial, and local governments inducing them to experiment with innovative economic development methods and structures.

As economic development established itself as a widely accepted and high-profile activity of local governments, these governments have more aggressively pursued their development goals. This has, in turn, made economic development a complex and challenging field. Public sector collaboration with private entities to enhance local economies has, for example, become less the anomaly and more the norm. The creation and management of these relationships are now a crucial part of the economic developer's job.

In response to this salience and complexity, many colleges and universities now offer courses and programs in economic development.

Professional certification training has mushroomed in every subject area from general economic development to small business incubation. Although some practitioners have no formal training, their numbers are steadily dwindling.

Despite increased sophistication of the profession, local economic development continues to be narrowly focused on one goal: job-creation. This is politically understandable since jobs are a tangible outcome politicians can proudly point to when defending their records. Low unemployment wins votes. Yet economic development includes much more than job-creation. In fact, job-creation may merely be the end product of a well-considered, comprehensive, and rational approach to economic development. In other words, if the process is done well, the jobs will follow.

Still more thought must be given to the secondary and long-term effects of local development activities and to the way in which economic development plans fit within the broader perspective of community development. In doing so, economic development professionals can play a vital role in mitigating the persistent inner city and rural poverty previously referred to.

WHY PLAN FOR ECONOMIC DEVELOPMENT?

In a market economy, a set of forces translates the desires of individuals into an allocation of productive resources. Because market forces are so complex, intervention in the market by government can be risky, and often produces results that are the opposite of those intended. Some will argue that in the context of a national market economy, a local economy will function on its own and should receive a minimal amount of local government intervention. They may further argue that if a particular community's economy does poorly, it is because natural market forces are drawing people and business to other regions of the nation, and that this shift is good for the national economy.

However, the notion that the private economy should be left alone assumes that markets behave according to the economist's model of perfect competition. This model is based on some improbable postulates. The perfect market economy model assumes perfect communication between market participants, no externalities, a very large number of standardized items or units for sale, and a large enough number of buyers and sellers such that no participant can distort the market. In reality, private markets are full of imperfections that distort their automatic functioning for the good of all. The existence of these market imperfections does not necessarily argue against a market economy. One argument for local economic development planning may be, however, that the local government should take action to perfect the markets and make them work more efficiently.

Another argument for economic development planning is that local governments are already deeply involved in local business activity as suppliers of infrastructure, as tax collectors, and as regulators of land, building, and activities. Therefore any local government should, at the least, understand what effect its behavior has on the local economy.

A third argument for local economic development planning is that communities are in competition with one another. Although some dislocations may result from excessive intercommunity competition, this "mercantilism" also creates some benefits. The fact remains that our local governmental structure puts local economies head to head in a battle for economic survival. Those cities, metropolitan areas, rural regions, and states that do not plan effectively will lose.

At a minimum, therefore, local economic development planning continues to be important because it offers a strategy for improving the necessary interaction between business and government, for perfecting the markets through better communication, and for effectively competing for economic resources in a highly competitive environment.

PURPOSE OF THIS BOOK

The purpose of this book is to provide a framework for formulating an economic development plan for a local community. The book assumes that the plan is short-term and action-oriented, but designed to fit into long-range economic development planning and broader community planning. The community that employs this framework can be any size, from a well-organized neighborhood in a large city to a multicounty rural region. While the conceptual framework can apply to all kinds of economic development planning, the book is not oriented toward national planning in developing countries. The book provides a sound framework for theoretical research in economic development planning, but it is not simply a report on the results of a specific research effort.

The book is primarily designed for use by economic development practitioners. This may include employees of planning offices responsible for economic development planning, economic development and community development offices in local and regional governments, non-profit development organizations, economic development offices of utility companies, and private consultants to all of the above.

ORGANIZATION OF THIS BOOK

The outline of the book follows the steps of the rational planning and management processes and the problem-solving approach. Those steps are: (1) definition of measurable objective(s); (2) study and analysis; (3) plan formulation; (4) implementation; and (5) evaluation. The first chapter looks at the objectives of economic development planning and suggests a broader conception of them than is typically applied in practice. Because many people have difficulty defining meaningful objectives, the chapter provides some easy methods. It also discusses the way in which economic development objectives relate to other community goals.

The second and third chapters focus on the information needed to plan effectively for economic development and describe several categories of information. First of all, Chapter 2 discusses data required to evaluate progress toward measurable objectives. Second, the chapter lists basic information about the community organized according to needs of the private firm. Third, it examines information necessary to analyze needs of the local economy. The chapter emphasizes that the economic development planner should act frugally in allocating time and effort to data collection. The chapter points out how to collect only critical information, and how to determine the worth of data collection efforts.

Chapter 3 provides information about the public-private partnership tools available in the United States. Local economic development is really a partnership between the public sector and the private sector, and governments at all levels have developed a set of increasingly innovative approaches to this partnership. This chapter provides a framework within which specific programs can be designed. The first part of the chapter defines public-private partnerships. The second part discusses organizational structures used in the economic development process. The third part looks at specific activities or ways to establish partnerships. The outline of part three of Chapter 3 matches somewhat that of the "Needs of the Firm" section of Chapter 2. This is to reinforce the link between governmental action, on the one hand, and the needs of the business community, on the other hand, in the partnership process.

The fourth chapter relates how to translate objectives (normative information) and data (descriptive information) into a program of action (policy). It presents a variety of specific local economic development programs. Some of these are typically found in communities; some are not so typical. Herein lies the most dramatic difference between this second edition of the book and the original. The programs selected for presentation in this edition reflect changes, both subtle and significant, that have taken place in the local economic development arena since the early 1990s. They are intended to provide examples of the latest thinking in this policy field. The presentations of the selected programs share a common outline, including a description of the program, how it works, its advantages to businesses and to the community, and its costs.

Chapter 5 closes the loop of the planning cycle with a description of program evaluation. It discusses methods of continuous evaluation and feedback. The chapter ends with a treatment of the cross-impact matrix, a method of evaluation and program selection that provides continuity in evaluation and involvement by participants.

Chapter 6 serves to summarize and integrate the material presented throughout.

1

Objectives of the Economic Development Program

Since unemployment rates have declined in many parts of the country, we can begin thinking more carefully about the real goals of economic development planning. Although job-creation is always important, it makes sense in most contexts to ask what kinds of jobs we want to create. In some communities, other objectives of economic development planning are as important or more important than short-range job-creation.

The first step toward formulating an economic development action plan is to set measurable objectives. It is important to clarify why economic development is important so as to guide future action. The purpose of this chapter is to discuss how to establish meaningful and measurable economic development objectives in a political environment, and how to relate those to other planning and community development activities. The first section considers various objectives that communities may wish to attain through an economic development program. The second section provides instructions in setting measurable economic development objectives.

A VARIETY OF ECONOMIC DEVELOPMENT GOALS

Communities may have a variety of economic development objectives. Among those are job-creation, job retention, tax-base creation, increase in property values, retention of wealth, the reduction of poverty, economic stability, and economic self-sufficiency. It may, in fact, be wise for a community to pursue a combination of these. Several possible objectives are discussed below.

Job-Creation

A common goal of economic development planning is job-creation. Job-creation is a concern of local officials and the general public. People sense that a relationship exists between employment and other concerns such as property values, property taxes, and downtown business. This goal is supported by federal and state programs that place specific emphasis on job-creation. The U.S. Small Business Administration, for example, guides local certified development corporations to give loans only in situations where at least one job will be created for every $15,000 of loan. The now defunct federal Urban Development Action Grant Program used $15,000 as the level of grant offered per job created. When states use the Small Cities Community Development Block Grant Program for economic development activities, they also follow guidelines of about $15,000 per job created.

Job-creation seems to be a natural choice for an economic development objective because it appears, on the surface, easy to measure. But problems are inherent in an economic development program that focuses exclusively on job-creation. For instance, the willingness of people to commute long distances means that jobs created within a community may be filled by people from other communities. Or, jobs "created" by one jurisdiction might have naturally gone to a neighboring jurisdiction, resulting in no net benefit to the state, region, or nation involved.

When job-creation is accepted as an important goal of economic development planning, it usually makes sense to focus job-creation by occupation and industry rather than to pursue jobs at random. Recruiting businesses that match the labor skills readily available in the community will likely be more productive than enticing a business that must look outside the area to recruit qualified workers, while leaving many local people unemployed.

Job Retention

One problem with job-creation as an objective of economic development planning is its inherent unfairness to existing businesses. It promotes a situation wherein the new business experiences an advantage over existing businesses. Theoretically, one job retained within a community benefits the community as much as one new job created. Job retention is much harder to measure, however, since the threat of a firm to leave town or cease operations is difficult to assess.

Roger Vaughn and Robert Pollard of Vaughn Associates, and Barbara Dyer of the Council of State Planning Agencies claim that people too often confuse both job-creation and job retention with economic development. They state that many public programs that focus on numbers of jobs in the name of economic development actually inhibit wealth creation and development. They demonstrate, for example, that efforts to attract new export industries into the community using local resources may be subsidizing outside buyers at the expense of local businesses, thus causing wealth to flow out of the community (Vaughn, Pollard, and Dyer, 1985).

Tax-Base Creation

Another economic development goal often pursued is tax-base creation. The pressure to create additional tax base is always apparent because of the pressure on political leaders to hold the line on taxes. Politicians want to have resources to accomplish new projects and programs, but would like to finance these new initiatives with natural revenue growth. Consciously or unconsciously, tax-base creation becomes a prominent reason for pursuing economic development in communities such as suburban municipalities where a high percentage of their breadwinners are employed in neighboring communities.

Although a relevant and legitimate goal, tax-base creation induces a set of actions different from that of job-creation. Whereas job-creation efforts promote a search for labor-intensive activities, the effect of a tax-base creation goal depends on what tax revenue source is most important for a community. Most commonly, tax-base creation causes a push for capital-intensive firms. Since most communities and local school systems rely heavily on real property taxation, many economic development coordinators look for real estate development prospects such as suburban office building and hotel projects. In many industrial communities in personal property tax states, the personal property base is as large as the real property base, with most of the personal property found in the two or three largest industrial establishments. Therefore, economic development often means seeking large-scale, labor-intensive industrial development projects.

In states with local sales tax options, a tax-base creation objective

results in the attraction of large numbers of commercial establishments. In California, where Proposition 13 has put pressure on localities to raise revenues from sources other than the property tax,
attracting a large number of fast food franchises may be considered the
accomplishment of economic development goals.

Increase in Property Values

Increasing the value of existing real property may be another potential economic development goal for reasons other than tax-base creation. It is often promoted by a community's power structure because
many members of the community's elite own large amounts of real estate. Controlling property values is, however, a tricky business. While
one may assume that economic growth increases the value of existing
property, property values are actually highly dependent upon *situs* considerations as well as the strength of the regional economy. Rapid economic growth may increase property values in the short run, but
maintaining a high quality of living is the best guarantor of long-term
property value growth.

Retention of Wealth

Retaining wealth in the local community may be the bottom line for
economic development planning. Generating large numbers of jobs may
be wheel-spinning if a high percentage of the wealth resulting from
that income quickly leaves town. Wealth leaves town via many routes,
such as through local residents who spend a high percentage of their
income outside the community. Local business and industry do little to
promote the retention of wealth in a community if most of the inputs
to their production process are purchased outside the community. Even
investing one's savings can cause wealth to leave the community tem-
porarily if those investments are in other parts of the country or the
world.

This objective focuses more on promoting local savings, investment,
and entrepreneurship than promoting growth from the outside.

Reduction of Poverty

Poverty reduction is difficult for any local government to pursue. Because people are so mobile, highly successful projects to reduce poverty

in one community could have the effect of attracting more poor to it from other communities. Poverty remains a national problem in need of a national solution.

If poverty reduction is a local economic development goal, it must be attacked on a broad front. One approach is through employment, but this means more than providing jobs. The first step is to provide the health and personal services needed to allow an unemployed person to become employable. The next step is to develop basic abilities such as math and reading skills. This needs to be followed by a program that provides the unemployed with an understanding of the culture of the world of work, which can then be followed by vocational skill development. Job placement and career advancement assistance must also be included. The chain of events may require several months or years for some low-income individuals, and if the chain is broken at any point, one may have to start from scratch. Employment programs reach only part of the poverty population of any community, many of whom are not employable (Muth, Hamlin, and Stuhmer, 1979).

Economic Stability

An important economic development goal is to promote economic stability. Even when a community is growing, major dislocations result from highly cyclical development. Large firms ride out economic cycles. Individuals and families suffer through minor downswings with savings and unemployment compensation. Certain other sectors of the local economy are devastated by periodic busts. Small businesses, for example, have a tough time getting started in a highly cyclical local economy. A small business needs about six years of successful operation before it reaches a stable plateau. If a local economy experiences exaggerated effects of national economic cycles, local start-up businesses may never get off the ground.

Financial institutions also become more conservative in cyclical communities, and governments have greater difficulty financing capital projects necessary to develop the economy. Cyclical communities become more dependent on large industries and have little chance for diversification. These characteristics can be seen in Flint, Michigan, which is not a poor community, but one of the most cyclical in the nation.

Economic stability is obtained through employers who sell to a broad spectrum of markets. This does not mean simply a smattering of types of business, but a set of businesses that are variously affected by the economic vicissitudes of the outside world (see "Needs of the Local Economy" in Chapter 2). Setting a goal of economic stability requires an understanding of markets and linkages. An economic stability objective may be to increase sales and employment by firms that are countercyclical to the dominant firm of the community.

Economic Self-Sufficiency

One way to conserve wealth and promote economic stability is to promote local self-sufficiency. Clearly, total self-sufficiency is seldom possible. In fact, making ties with the outside world to generate exports is one of the goals of community economic development. Community self-sufficiency really means minimizing imports from other parts of the country.

One significant import is energy. Few communities supply their own fossil fuels. In the typical community, 100 percent of its energy is imported. Because energy costs are such a significant part of the budgets of households, industries, and governments, even small percentage gains in energy conservation are meaningful. They imply large amounts of money retained in the community that would have otherwise drained off to other regions.

Agriculture represents a possible area for greater self-sufficiency. Many major industrial areas are surrounded by rich agricultural regions. Often their products pass through several hands and travel many miles before returning to the same community for consumption.

Reducing intermediaries can increase local farmer profits, reduce local food prices, and retain more money in the community. Creating farmers' markets, linking restaurants with farms for direct produce production, and establishing local food processing and packaging businesses are ways to promote local agricultural self-sufficiency.

Complementarity

It is important to ensure that the economic development objectives identified by a local community be complementary to one another. As is evidenced by the discussion of individual objectives above, there is always the danger that in the wrong "mix," objectives may cancel each other out or work in combination to have a perverse effect on the local economy.

A good understanding of the tools of public intervention in the private market and their effects on private firms and individual behavior can help the economic development professional to recommend objectives that will work positively and synergistically for community-wide development.

ESTABLISHING MEASURABLE ECONOMIC DEVELOPMENT OBJECTIVES

Objectives are statements that serve as a guide for action. They are something to shoot for. Measurable objectives have the following additional characteristics:

1. They can be achieved.
2. The time of their achievement can be determined.
3. Progress toward their achievement can be measured.

Example of a Measurable Economic Development Objective

If an economic development goal is to broaden the local economic base so as to mitigate the cyclical impact of recessions, a measurable objective might be "to cause employment to expand by 4,000 in a set of identified countercyclical industries."

To make this objective operational, "countercyclical" must be carefully defined. It could mean industries that have cycles opposite those of the dominant local industry. The word "cause" is included in the objective statement because in order to evaluate the worth of the economic development program, we are interested in knowing the impact of the program itself. The stated objective is achievable: its achievement can be measured, and intermediate levels of achievement can be determined.

Why Establish Measurable Objectives?

Inducing individuals to think carefully about the future is always difficult. Motivating people to define measurable objectives is even more difficult. Most do not know what is achievable, and they do not like to be put in a position in which they might fail. Political leaders are particularly uncomfortable in being specific about goals, even though they have to be specific about dollars and laws. It requires a mode of thinking to which people are unaccustomed.

However, creating and implementing economic development programs are expensive undertakings. One must understand the impact of actions to determine if the dividends are worth the investment.

Defining measurable objectives:

- forces people to think more precisely about their actions
- generates positive discussion
- provides a benchmark of success for periodic evaluation of directions and actions
- helps participants put the mundane day-to-day activities of economic development into a larger context
- offers daily feedback on progress so as to provide both a stimulant to and a psychological reward for daily progress

How to Establish Measurable Objectives

Given the difficulty of encouraging people to establish measurable objectives, a special effort is required to get them built into the economic development plan. The following are some suggestions for making the process work more smoothly.

1. Establish an advisory group for the economic development program whose job it is to set measurable objectives, and monitor progress toward them.
2. Keep the group small (about five) so as to promote discussion.
3. Meet regularly, but for short periods of time (about once a month, over breakfast or lunch).
4. Have one or two elected officials on the group, but do not make it all elected officials.
5. Ensure that two or three different sectors of the business and general communities are represented.
6. Survey outside groups before discussing objectives. If possible, complete a community opinion survey in order to give the group

Figure 1.1
Format for Writing Measurable Objectives

1. OBJECTIVE NUMBER _____	
2. short title	
3. OBJECTIVE	
4. definitions	
5. 75% attainment of objective	
6. 50% attainment of objective	
7. data needed to measure progress:	8. source:
9. ramifications and secondary impacts of attainment	

a sense of community purpose (see "Business Retention Survey," Chapter 2).

7. Discuss and formulate about five to ten measurable objectives that can be achieved in the next year.

8. Establish data collection procedures to ensure data availability to evaluate progress. Multiyear goals should be broken down into one-year objectives.

9. Reevaluate objectives at least once a year.

The form in Figure 1.1 provides a suggestion as to how each objective should be written. On line (1) in Figure 1.1 give the objective a number, and on line (2), a short title. Both are for the purpose of quick reference. On line (3) carefully state a complete, one-sentence objective. On line (4) provide an elaboration of any terms used in the objective. Lines (5) and (6) state what would constitute 75 percent and 50 percent attainment. The ability to write these intermediate targets is a check to see if the original objective is in workable form. Line (7) lists quantitative information required to evaluate achievement of the objective and line (8) offers a source for that information. Line (9) holds a brief statement of the effects of accomplishing the objective.

SUMMARY

The first step in the planning process is to set measurable objectives. Objectives should be measurable so as to motivate and sharpen community discussion, and to be able to monitor progress. Typically, economic development is defined as creating jobs in a community, but we should begin thinking about a broader array of reasons for and kinds of economic development. Improving economic conditions in many communities allows us to plan for economic development more carefully.

2

Inventory of the Local Economic Situation

After defining measurable objectives, the second step in the action plan process is to inventory the local economic situation. This step involves data collection and analysis. Once more is known about the local economy, measurable objectives may be revised based on this improved understanding. This is appropriate since the entire process is iterative and dynamic rather than a static five-step sequence (see Figure 2.1). Goal formulation comes first because it acts as a guide to determine the kind of information that is needed.

This chapter describes methods of collecting and analyzing information for economic development planning. The first section demonstrates how to focus data collection efforts. The second section lists and briefly describes important categories of information. The list is organized in the same manner as a business firm might assess its own needs. The successful economic development planner must think in terms of those needs. The third section covers the importance of a business retention survey as a source of critical information, and the fourth section talks about analyzing the needs of the local economy.

PARSIMONIOUS DATA COLLECTION

Formulating a long list of useful information for local economic development planning is quite easy. Planners with a background in quan-

Figure 2.1
Dynamic Planning Process

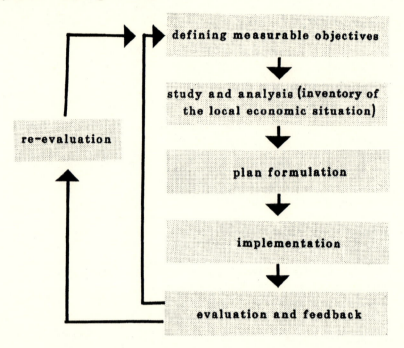

titative analysis quickly list figures on employment by firm, industry, and occupation. With this information, economic base analysis, shift/share analysis, and input-output analysis can be completed. Some items in this long list of information are readily available while others require substantial work.

However, data collection is expensive and data analysis is time consuming. One is easily overwhelmed with the economic information that can be collected in any community. It is common for valuable time to be spent obtaining data that are never fully analyzed and utilized in the planning process. Planners who are action oriented will want to be frugal in spending resources for data collection and analysis. RATHER THAN WORKING HARD TO COLLECT DATA, ONE SHOULD WORK HARD TO MINIMIZE DATA COLLECTION.

In order for data collection to be worthwhile the information must have these characteristics:

1. It must be worth collecting periodically and consistently, so as to become a part of a continuously functioning management information system.

2. It should have an immediate analytical use that leads directly to economic development decision-making.

The following three items represent a guide to parsimonious data collection that allows one to get on with the process of economic development:

1. Collect information that relates to established measurable objectives.

2. Collect information about the needs of firms.

3. Collect information that helps the local economy respond to the needs of the outside world.

Each of these three items is discussed in the following sections.

LINK TO MEASURABLE OBJECTIVES

Measurable objectives help outline what information is most critical. If measurable objectives are clearly defined, and the objective sheets filled in carefully, the information called for on line (7) in Figure 1.1 may be all the information that is needed to operate an effective economic development program. Depending on the resources available, this information becomes the basis for a computerized or manual management information system for the economic development office.

NEEDS OF THE FIRM

The second most important data to be collected is information that satisfies the needs of local and prospective businesses. Public planners, who are often educated in a public sector mode, do not always have a clear understanding of private sector culture. Without the experience of actually running a business, one cannot develop a real internal understanding of how the hopes and anxieties of the business person govern business behavior. The phrase "cash flow," for example, does not

Table 2.1
Needs and Concerns of the Firm

1. Land
2. Labor
3. Capital
4. Energy
5. Finance
6. Management
7. Taxes
8. Research
9. Quality of life

take on true meaning for those who have not been "baptized" with the emotions of many sleepless nights.

To compensate for this lack of "gut-level" understanding, economic development planners must attempt to orient their thinking to the needs of the firm. In this way they can relate to the businessperson's perspective and can better understand how their community does or does not satisfy those needs. This helps the planner to understand both how to attract new businesses to the community and how to promote those that already exist. The information can also be used in community promotional information.

Table 2.1 provides a list of the general categories of the needs of the firm, not necessarily in order of priority. The meaning of each of the items is described thereafter, along with important information the economic development planner should keep on file, ready to communicate to the business community. Sources of this information are listed in Table 2.2 at the end of this section.

Land

Land means more than a piece of real estate. It means usable, accessible space to develop new facilities. A major attraction to a firm looking for a new location is the existence of land that can be built upon quickly. This means infrastructure completed, ready for use, and adequate for future growth. Water, sewer, storm drainage, pavement, curbs, and gutters should all be in place. The land should be accessible to transportation systems; it should be flat for industrial development, and have good soils for development. The prospective business should not have to deal with any legal delays before construction. Zoning should be taken care of and property liens discharged. Outstanding land contracts, second mortgages, deed restrictions, and so on should be disposed of.

Moreover, there should be a choice of such parcels because one single location cannot fit the needs of a variety of business types.

A fundamental data element is, therefore, a list of available parcels of property indicating ownership, possible use, and status with respect to all of the issues mentioned above, maintained in the form of a land availability data bank. Some of this information already exists in the tax assessor's office and in planning reports, but not all of it is in the detail required. The local economic development professional may need to assemble this information from a variety of sources as described in Table 2.2.

Land availability also carries importance for existing businesses. One of a local community's most important resources is the successful local business. They are a rare find, but highly successful businesses inevitably have expansion problems. Often the local community does not even hear about their expansion problem, and the business does not realize the community can help. The business is landlocked, looks around, does not see adequate expansion or relocation alternatives, and moves on. Later, the local city government hears that a former local fledgling business is now booming somewhere else. In one midwestern community, for example, a tool and die company located in a small unimpressive building left town. It was not until late in the process that the local government learned that the tool and die operation used laser technology, had substantial federal contracts, was nearly debt free, and was leaving town because it could not find expansion space.

When expansion can be handled by adding onto existing facilities, keeping lines of communication open is still important. As an information broker, the economic developer might be able to assist in real estate trades and zoning changes. Expansion of one firm might be connected with the relocation of another. If relocation is necessary, the land availability data bank will serve existing business as well as prospective ones.

A truly proactive economic developer will monitor businesses in his or her community so as to remain up to date on their needs for land.

Table 2.2
Inventory Data Sources

Needs of the Firm	Data Sources
Land	1. local urban planning office
	2. local assessor's office
	3. municipal zoning map
	4. survey of local firms
	5. local realtors
	6. Recorder of Deeds office
	7. utilities serving the area
Labor	**Census Materials**
	1. Census of Manufactures
	2. Census of Retail Trade
	3. Census of Wholesale Trade
	4. County Business Patterns
	5. City-County Data Book
	6. Census of Population
	Other Sources
	7. regional planning commission or COG
	8. state employment security office
	9. area community college or university
Physical Capital	1. local realtors
	2. state and county highway depts.
	3. railroads serving the area
	4. trucking firms serving the area
	5. local or regional transportation authorities
	6. utilities
	7. communication providers
	8. municipal building depts.

This kind of data can be collected on a regular basis through mail or telephone surveys or by local realtors. It can also be added to the land availability data bank to facilitate matching needs with availability.

Labor

Difficulties in maintaining an affordable, stable, and productive labor force represent some of the most frustrating experiences for the businessperson. It is an area in which she/he feels most helpless. Therefore, a firm thinking of a new location will check out the characteristics of the labor market very thoroughly. In fact, Roger Schmenner found that

Table 2.2 (*cont.*)

Needs of the Firm	Data Sources
Energy	1. utilities
	2. municipal building and zoning depts.
	3. area universities
	4. survey of local businesses
Finance	1. *Directory of Incentives for Business Investment and Development in the United States*
	2. *Site Selection Handbook*
	3. area SBA offices
	4. state government economic development agency
	5. local banks
Management	1. local SBA offices
	2. area community college or university
	3. local chamber of commerce
	4. local business incubator/business development centers
	5. special districts
Quality of Life	1. local chamber of commerce
	2. state economic development agency
	3. *Places Rated Almanac*

76 percent of the respondents to a business survey of constraints on the choice of state or regional location for a new plant cited a favorable labor climate as a "must" (Schmenner, 1982, p. 150). The economic development planner needs good information on and a thorough understanding of the labor market.

Labor force concerns of the firm can be divided into four major categories: (1) size; (2) stability; (3) skills; and (4) cost. Each of these categories, and their relation to different types of firms, will be discussed in turn.

Labor Force Size and Mobility

An adequate labor supply is important to business. One determines the overall size by tabulating the number of labor force participants living within commuting distance of the business (see Figure 2.2). This may go far beyond the jurisdiction of the economic development professional. Commuting distances are measured in time-distance, and are somewhat greater for professional employees than for blue-collar work-

Figure 2.2
Labor Market Area Map

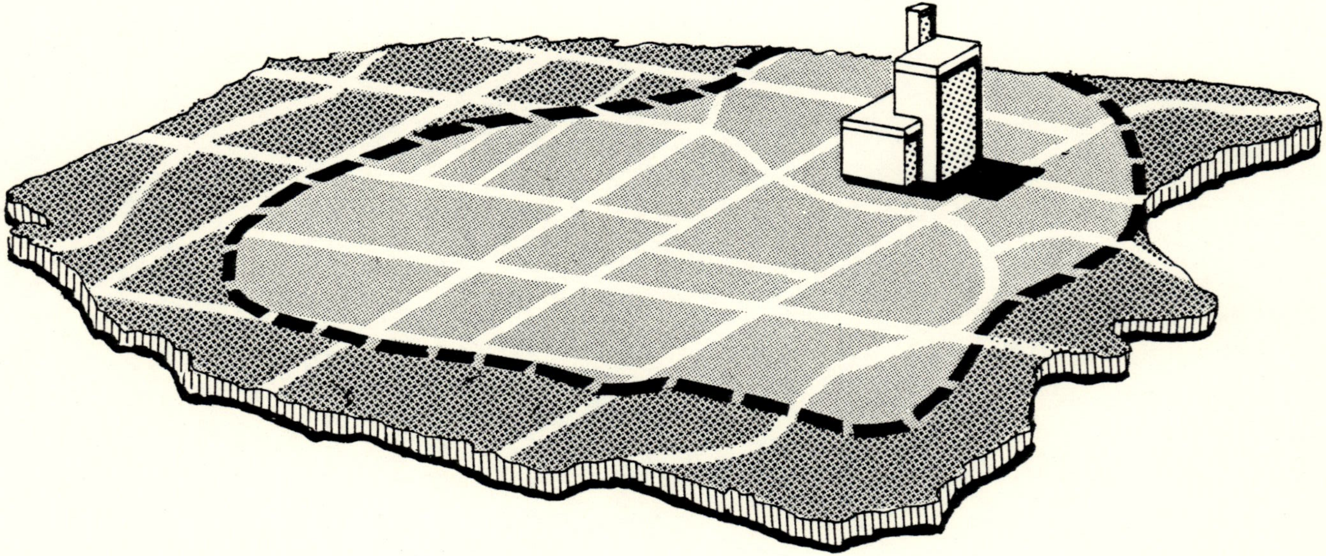

COMPANY X

ers. Professional employees in major metropolitan areas are known to commute up to two hours one way. A more conservative labor market estimate would put commuting distance at approximately 1¼ hours. This can be reduced to approximately one hour for semiskilled and unskilled workers.

Although the above figures refer to automobile driving time, as much as 20 percent of the unskilled labor force may be transit dependent. Firms that are not located on a transit line, but employ large amounts of unskilled labor, may find themselves at a disadvantage. Similarly, a community that does not link such firms with mass transit, or guide those firms to a location with transit service, may find that it has an unemployment problem despite abundant employment opportunities.

The low end of the clerical labor market represents another sector in which transit is important. Many firms complain of a shortage of clerical help even in the worst of economic times. One-car families with two breadwinners often have transportation problems.

Stability and Work Habits

Stability means that the firm can depend on employees to show up regularly, be well behaved, attentive, and alert. A stable workforce in the eyes of many firms is one with a high work ethic, few strikes, and few personal problems.

Labor problems are human interaction problems complicated by the most basic of human concerns: money, time, work environment, and distance from home. For employers always to get their way in employee relations would be unfair, but industrial firms are clearly disenchanted with communities with a reputation for labor instability. An ever increasing number of firms are seeking communities with reputations for high labor stability and good work habits.

Skills

This category refers to the talents, training, and abilities of employees, whether these skills were acquired in basic educational programs, vocational education, work experience, or elsewhere. The development professional cannot keep track of the number of labor force participants with certain skills, but an understanding of the general level of education of the community can be very important.

Large industrial firms. Labor market planners often talk about the need to train the labor force to meet the needs of potential industry. Considerable evidence indicates, however, that the vocational skills of the labor force are one of the lesser concerns of major industrial firms, such as those manufacturers employing more than 500 employees. Many industrialists maintain that if they can be provided with a stable workforce, they can do the rest. Major firms are often not interested in a workforce with a high level of specialized vocational training because they have the resources to do training themselves, and they may feel they can do a better job. Their semiskilled jobs are often quite specialized, and quickly become obsolete. Their machinery is often designed especially for the use of their industrial operation with little carryover from one company to the next (Muth, Hamlin, and Stuhmer, 1979).

Where skills are a problem to industrialists, their concern is finding employees well grounded in the basic skills required to read instructions, measure, and do simple mathematical manipulations. The economic development planner should know the basic skill level of his or her community. Does the local labor force have a reading problem? Many do. Are local firms finding that employees do not have the ability to do simple mathematical manipulations? Do major industrial firms find it necessary to incorporate some basic skill training into their on-the-job training? Many do. Does the local community, state, or region have a reputation for a labor force with poor basic education? What programs exist in the community to improve basic skills? Are such programs run by the school system, the local community college, or nonprofit groups? Are they working?

Small businesses. Smaller businesses, meaning those of twenty employees or fewer, take a different perspective about the needs of the labor market. They do not have the resources to invest in training, and may not have so many specialized employee positions. They cannot afford to train employees for several months. The location and survival of a small manufacturing operation may be heavily dependent on the ability of the firm to find skilled labor.

The economic development planner should know what training is available. Successful economic development programs have well-established linkages between vocational programs and small business needs. In this way expanding businesses and new businesses can be assured that coordinated training will provide skilled employees.

Cost

Labor cost refers to the total dollars a firm must pay to receive the services of employees. The economic developer should know the prevailing wage for various occupations. This information is mandatory when communities become involved in federal programs for which Davis-Bacon applies. Knowing how local wage rates compare with those of other regions of the country may also be helpful.

Labor costs include far more than salaries and wages, however. Fringe benefits are one of the biggest differentiations in cost between regions. Benefits can cost between 15 and 35 percent of the base wage. Many benefits offered to employees are determined by the firm or are the result of labor negotiations. These generally include life insurance, health insurance, disability insurance, and dental insurance. The level of cost for some fringes, such as worker's compensation, depends on state law even where handled through private carriers. Unemployment compensation may be dependent on state law as well as federal law. In those states with unemployment compensation funds that are in debt to the federal government, a surcharge known as a solvency tax is levied against employers.

Many companies feel fringes have gotten out of hand for two reasons: first, many of the standard parts of a fringe package, such as health care, have risen in price at faster-than-expected rates, and, second, government-mandated fringes, such as worker's compensation, unemployment compensation, and FICA are quite high. In some northeastern and midwestern states, labor-intensive service firms are concerned more with the high price of worker's and unemployment compensation than with high state income taxes. High worker's compensation costs and high unemployment compensation costs were the second and third most negative aspects of doing business in the state, according to 1,592 Michigan industrial firms surveyed by Michigan Bell Telephone Company in 1986 and 1987. In the 1990s the state legislature targeted those issues for change so as to improve the state's competitiveness.

Fringe benefits are particularly burdensome for a small firm or new venture because of administrative costs and the lack of volume discounts common to fringe packages. One solution to this problem is fringe-benefit pooling for small businesses, in which several firms share the same fringe program. Local insurance agents are currently offering pooling programs in many communities on a limited basis.

Physical Capital

The next major need of firms to be considered is physical capital. Physical capital means the physical building, machinery, equipment, and infrastructure needed for business operation. In the Schmenner survey (referred to in the "Labor" section of this chapter), rail service, a location on the expressway, and the special provision of utilities were the three factors most commonly cited by respondents in final site selection (Schmenner, 1982, p. 150).

Building and Equipment

To the extent possible, the economic development office should keep track of available industrial and commercial buildings. The concerns for available space are similar to those discussed under "Land." Space must be ready for immediate occupancy. The economic development professional may also be involved in assisting prospective businesses in acquiring or leasing equipment. The federal government has title to a large amount of heavy equipment that it acquired through foreclosures on Economic Development Administration (EDA) loans. Knowledge about this and similar sources helps and should be made part of the land availability data base referred to earlier in this chapter.

Regional Transportation

The importance of public sector capital equals that of private capital. Transportation systems, both public and private, are the most visible of the infrastructure needs.

Highways. Because of the importance of accessibility to business location, it is necessary to calculate the time-distance from parts of the region to other critical points. It is helpful to know what highways are in the planning stage because of the impact they will have. A prospective business would be wise to investigate load limits and responsibility for care of major highways in the area. The economic development director should have this information readily available.

Railroads and sidings. In addition to knowing the location of rail lines relative to commercial and industrial property, the economic development planner should know approximate cost per ton/mile for long-distance rail freight, where sidings are located, and how they are served.

Trucking. Information for trucking is similar to that for railroads. The economic developer needs to know what truckers serve the region, the location and servicing of their docks, and the approximate cost per ton/mile of long-distance freight.

Air transportation. Air transportation means a variety of things to the modern business. It refers to airline passenger transportation, private passenger service, and freight. Industrial firms are gravitating to airports, and air industrial parks have been one of the most successful kinds of industrial parks in the last two decades. The ability of the company executive to get in and out quickly of meetings and plant tours explains much of the attraction to airports, perhaps more so than the convenience of the plant to freight transportation. The capacity to taxi the company plane up to the plant door offers an irresistible luxury. When it is impossible for a community to have an air industrial park or even an airport, other efforts must be made to ensure that the community's air transportation situation is competitive. Express passenger ground transportation service to the nearest airport is crucial to communities of all sizes and air freight rates and facilities should be monitored by the economic development planner.

Pipelines. Improvements in interstate pipeline technology are continuously expanding the spectrum of products that they can transport. Pipelines should be treated in the same way as any mode of freight transportation. They have a terminal and a line haul. Businesses need to know how they can obtain access to them and how much they cost.

Water and Sewer

Many industrial operations are big water users, and large office buildings requiring heavy air conditioning also have large water demands. The cost of water varies widely. In some communities it is free. In most communities water is billed by a meter, and water bills can constitute a major portion of the cost of production. Water rate structures may be as complex as energy rate structures. The economic developer should understand the water costs that local businesses face and how their water rates compare with those of other communities, so as to provide firms with essential information.

In some cases water rates are high because sewage is not separately metered. Water meter readings are simply doubled to cover the cost of wastewater treatment on the assumption that all water that goes into a parcel of property will come out in another form. For the industrial firm that consumes water in production and discharges it as steam, this billing system may be unfair. In the opposite direction, some firms extract water from their own well, contaminate it in the production process and then dump the wastewater into the municipal system. These firms need to have their wastewater separately metered and billed.

In smaller communities, the largest two or three industries in town may consume more water than all of the houses combined, and may also produce more wastewater. Industrial wastewater with high pH levels and greater suspended solids may require more stages of treatment to meet state water quality standards. In some states and communities, a firm that places a heavy burden on the wastewater system is asked to make a special contribution to the cost of expanding the wastewater treatment plant or to build a pre-treatment facility on its own site to reduce the burden on the municipal plant. A pre-treatment facility could cost several million dollars.

Regional Communications Systems

Business firms are finding communication technology to be increasingly important in making locational decisions. Generally, we think of advanced communications as allowing more flexibility in business location as technology reduces the "friction of space." Yet information technology is changing so rapidly that many communities have difficulty keeping up. Geographic regions with small backward local telephone companies have difficulty attracting and keeping industry. Lack of services that many take for granted can cause frustration for corporate executives. Living without cell phone service feels prehistoric to those who consider it second nature, for example. As extranet and business-to-business internet connections become essential to business operations, locations without at least Ethrnet, cable modems, or other high-speed connections will also find business retention and attraction difficult.

In the long run, the communications revolution will make firms more footloose. As the product of U.S. business becomes more abstract and information-oriented, rather than physical and industrial, and as communication technology reduces the need for transportation for many management functions, business in the United States will be more free to locate in small communities and out-of-the-way places. However, in the near future, business reliance on advanced communication technologies may have a centripetal effect. The desire to be close to the services described above can act as a powerful force of attraction for firms, just as expressway interchanges or regional airports have in the recent past. By way of comparison, the interstate highway system is presently more geographically dispersed than many of the popular advanced communication technologies.

Economic development planners must maintain current information on any and all of these forms of physical capital that are relevant to exchange networks with other departments of the local government, state and national departments and agencies, and utilities that serve the area.

Energy

Energy is a major component in the locational decisions of some types of firms. How each firm views energy differs, but two kinds of concerns are cost and stability.

Cost

One obvious concern is that cost and rate structures can be complex. The economic developer should have precise knowledge of electrical and natural gas rate structures. While some parts of the country have flat rates per kilowatt hour for electricity and per cubic meter for gas, other areas have graduated rates. Some also have seasonal rates. In most cases, commercial and industrial firms pay a rate different from that of residential customers.

It is equally important to know the ownership of the energy source because different ownership patterns will have varying regulatory and political implications. Does a municipal power source, a cooperative, or a private firm own the utility? It may also be important to have some knowledge of the mix of sources from which power comes, because the price of various sources of energy fluctuate relative to one another over time. Does the local utility receive its power primarily from hydropower, coal generation, or a nuclear power plant?

How are utility rates set? Does the local utility justify every rate change before a state public service commission, or does a fuel cost adjustment clause in its charter allow automatic price increases when fuel costs rise? The nation is now implementing competition in the sales of local power, giving businesses a choice of energy retailers. What is the status of the local community and its state in terms of implementing local retail competition for energy?

Firms that generate some of their own power place importance on another issue. They may have a bank of solar cells, or may own a small dam with hydroelectric potential. Federal law requires that utilities buy back excess power from power generators, or allow firms to wheel power over utility lines from the power source to their industrial plant. These firms may be interested in knowing the buyback and wheeling rates.

Stability

In some cases, firms are more interested in the stability of power than its cost. In some industrial operations, a brownout or blackout lasting for a day or more may be disastrous. If the local utility has a bad record in that regard, its reputation could be a severe economic development disadvantage.

Finance

The secret of economic development, throughout all of human history, has been a magical and somewhat mystical process known as translating savings into investment. What this means in theoretical terms is that an individual defers the gratification of current consumption (savings) and applies it toward the creation of more efficient methods (investment) for better future production. In Robinson Crusoe's world, this means saving up food so that he can take one day off from hunting to sharpen his stone knife. This accumulation of capital allows him to hunt more effectively in the future.

In the modern jungle things are not so simple. Few businesses can effectively form from the savings of a single individual. They must pool the savings of large numbers of people. In fact, the financial needs of a firm do not stop when the business succeeds. They continue throughout the life of the business. Often, the more successful the business, the greater the need for financial assistance.

The organization that acts as a broker between savers and investors is called a financial intermediary. Common modern examples are banks, savings and loan associations, credit unions, the stock and bond markets, insurance companies, mutual funds, and money market funds. The economic success of any nation, society, or community is closely related to the quality of its financial intermediaries. The economic development professional should know the existence, attitudes, and policies of financial intermediaries that serve his or her community.

Merely listing banks that make business loans is not good enough. The financial needs of a firm vary by type of firm and according to the stage of its life cycle. Bank loans only provide financing for a small part of business financial needs. With respect to small businesses, banks are most accustomed to dealing with short-term working capital loans. These loans are small relative to net worth and are secured with inventory or other assets owned by the business. Personal guarantees by the principals are usually required for the three- to five-year loans. In recent years, the interest rate charged on such loans has been set at two to three percentage points over New York consensus prime, renegotiated periodically or automatically readjusted with movements in prime. Lower rates are available if the variable rate has no upper limit or if the loan is secured with real estate or long-life equipment.

Banks base approval of small business loans on past trends of business performance, cash-flow sufficiency, and collateral reserve. Local banks are not usually in the business of analyzing new business ideas or technologies and seldom make long-term business loans. If a community relies too heavily on local banks for business capital, it will find many of its small businesses constantly cash-poor and excessively vulnerable to movements in short-term interest rates. Idea firms, technology firms, and capital-intensive firms will be stifled. Failure to recognize the limits of bank financing greatly restricts the kind of business that can successfully operate in the community.

Two major gaps in traditional financing of small businesses are: (1) start-up or transition financing, and (2) long-term loans for long-life fixed assets. The following sections discuss each of these.

Start-up or Transition Capital

One of the most difficult forms of financing for a small business to obtain is start-up capital. This refers to money needed for the start-up of a new business, or for a major expansion of a successful business ready to enter a new phase of operation. At these points in its history, a business experiences costs in advance of increases in sales to cover costs. These costs include new machinery, equipment, and marketing. Without start-up capital, a revolutionary idea or product may die for lack of ability to convert to mass marketing and production. Communities that do not have start-up or transition capital available will be at a disadvantage in attracting new businesses or promoting the expansion of existing ones. The local economic development professional should know of the availability of local start-up capital so as to guide businesses in the right direction. Three kinds of start-up capital discussed below are seed capital, venture capital, and pre-venture capital. Each of these differs substantially in sources, uses, form, and capitalistic motive.

Seed capital. Seed capital provides money to a start-up business to overcome the initial hurdles of business formation until the business can generate its own working capital. The type of business looking for seed capital can be any of a wide variety, including small industrial, service, or retail. Seed capital can take the form of either debt or equity investment but usually offers a loan. It amounts to somewhere between $30,000 and $300,000 with a term of approximately five years. Seed capitalists require a high return on investment, because of the risk. They usually want approximately prime plus 10 percent. Seed capitalists can be banks, although banks are usually not equipped to perform this function and are reluctant to make high-risk loans. Local investors interested in a high rate of return on investment are often the best source. The local economic development professional should determine which individuals in the community are interested in making seed capital investments. Local governments or affiliated nonprofits may also make seed capital investments through a revolving fund for small business finance (see "Revolving Fund").

Westfield, Massachusetts, did a study of its own incubator industries to determine their characteristics. One discovery was that most start-up capital for these firms came from the personal equity of the business's principals (Mullin and Armstrong, 1983).

Venture capital. The term "venture capital" is popular these days, and many people confuse it with seed capital. Although they have very similar purposes, they differ in magnitude and in the actors involved. Designed for businesses with high growth potential, venture capital investments are large. They typically amount to over $1,000,000 and go to high-tech firms attempting to market a major new technological breakthrough. This invention gives the firm a technological monopoly for three to five years. Venture capital usually takes the form of equity injection through the purchase of company stock. Venture capitalists usually require substantial control over the company they are purchasing a share of so as to protect their investment.

Venture capitalists look for a return on their investment of 100 percent per year for about three years. This extremely high rate of return is required to offset losses that result in those cases of poor investment.

As an equity injection, venture capital does not have a term, but venture capitalists do not see themselves as permanent owners of the company. They typically want to sell out after about five years to free cash for other investments. They do this by selling the company to a larger corporation, selling back to the original inventor, or taking the business public.

Most venture capital companies are private companies, or subsidiaries of banks or insurance companies. Some wealthy individuals become involved in venture capital investments. The federal government has had a program since the 1950s to promote venture capital company creation. Many venture capital companies are formed under the Small Business Administration program called Small Business Investment Companies (SBIC). This program gives moderate-interest loans to companies that have raised over $1 million of private capital to be used in venture capital investments. The Minority Small Business Investment Company (MESBIC) program has somewhat less stringent private capital requirements but gives loans to companies that make venture investments only in minority businesses.

Although cities do not become involved in venture capital, states are becoming involved in increasing numbers. Several years ago, the state of Michigan passed a law allowing for the use of a portion of state pension fund money to make venture capital investments in high-tech firms, thus creating one of the largest venture capital pools in the world. The program has been successful both in terms of the economic growth it has created and in terms of its return on investment. As a result, other states have formed, or are considering forming, similar venture investment pools.

What can the local economic developer do about venture capital? She or he must learn to tie into the state program or seek out SBICs or private venture capitalists. Just by knowing a legitimate venture capital situation, and where to find venture capital, the economic development professional can be of great assistance.

However, the local community needs to have control over at least some funds to leverage investments from other sources. Having a revolving fund that participates in venture and seed capital investments is necessary to maintain this leverage. The community should establish such a fund using private investment and a for-profit organizational structure.

Pre-venture capital. Pre-venture capital is different from either seed or venture capital. Pre-venture capital finances research and development at the product development stage. This stage takes a new scientific discovery and, through further research, translates it into a marketable product. Pre-venture capital does not exist in many communities. Found mainly near major universities, pre-venture capitalists do not buy stock in and control of companies so much as they buy control of patents and product development rights. Pre-venture capital often comes from limited partnerships because of the early tax write-offs. Foundations and university endowments are also becoming involved.

Pre-venture investments are smaller than venture capital investments because they do not finance mass production machinery and equipment. Research is expensive, however. Pre-venture investments are even riskier than venture investments and the ultimate rate of return on a successful venture must be even higher. But, because the investment comes at such an early stage of product development, the pre-venture capitalist needs to be more patient in receiving that return. The pre-venture capitalist usually gets his return by selling patents and development rights to companies interested in mass producing the product.

Long-term capital. Large corporations can float bonds to obtain long-term fixed financing, but small firms find that loans of five to ten years are all that is available from banks. This situation became more severe as dramatic changes in interest rates in the late 1970s and early 1980s put many banks in a difficult position. Although rates have come down, real interest rates (interest rate less inflation rate) are even higher now. Many financial institutions have vowed never again to be caught so extended during a time of such volatility.

Perhaps the best solution to this problem involves the use of a certified development corporation loan. Certified development corporations, authorized under section 504 of the Small Business Act, induce banks to extend longer credit by supporting longer-term loans with second mortgages. Certified development companies exist in nearly every community. A multicounty or state certified development company can be approached in the absence of a local company. The most difficult requirement of the program demands that the real estate or long-life equipment financed with the program be owned by the operating small business or its alter ego. It prohibits lending money to passive investors to acquire assets to lease to others. An alter ego is a partnership with an ownership percentage identical to that of the operating corporation. The partnership owns the plant and equipment and leases it to the corporation. This rule allows individuals to gain the advantages of real estate ownership even though they are doing business as a corporation. Economic development officers should work closely with whatever certified development company functions in their area.

Management

Business management is an extensive subject. It includes such diverse topics as the human aspects of personnel management and the data analysis associated with financial administration. Because good business management is an intangible, it is often not considered to be as important as it should be. Many entrepreneurs do not give management skills adequate attention, and this neglect is considered a primary reason for the high level of small business failure. Often a community can do much to increase employment and economic activity by providing management assistance to businesses so as to reduce failure. This can sometimes be accomplished by running training workshops on practical management issues, such as taxation, finance, personnel management, fringe benefits, and marketing techniques. These activities are often provided by community colleges, universities, chambers of commerce, business incubators, and business development centers. The economic development coordinator's job may be primarily to direct business to the appropriate assistance.

Direct technical assistance is more difficult to come by since it is time consuming and often requires the expertise of highly paid individuals. University faculty and business consulting firms are reluctant to provide assistance to small businesses for fear that the failure of a business they are providing technical assistance to would hurt their reputation and may create legal liability. Small business failure is such a common occurrence that the risk is significant.

One source of valuable technical assistance is the pool of retired and semiretired business people in any community, who might be willing to share their experience on a part-time basis at relatively low cost. The U.S. Small Business Administration also runs a technical assistance program consisting of retired volunteers, known as the Service Corps of Retired Executives (SCORE).

Taxes

Local Property Taxes

Clearly, the local economic developer should have a complete understanding of the local property tax and should have that information in a form that can be communicated to existing and prospective businesses. This may seem straightforward: just know the tax rate. However, in most parts of the country a variety of factors make this complicated.

Boundaries. First of all, local governmental boundaries in some areas are so complicated it requires a major research effort to determine the taxing jurisdictions of a single piece of property. The parcel may be taxed by a city, a separate school district, a county, a transportation authority, and a local community college. In some suburban areas in the midwest, police, fire protection, drainage, mosquito abatement, and a host of other municipal services are provided by special purpose governments rather than the city government, and each has independent taxing power. The economic development director should be prepared to get exact tax information from the tax assessor for relevant property as a form of assistance to prospective businesses, and should have quick reference maps showing boundary lines of taxing jurisdictions.

Abatements. Thirty-three states have provision for commercial and/ or industrial property tax abatement. In most states the local level administers the abatement with authorization from state enabling legislation. Typically, any business that increases its real and personal property holdings within the local community for the purpose of promoting its business activity can apply for an abatement of property taxation on the new property. In other words, if an industry builds a $1-million expansion to its local plant, it can apply for an abatement on some part of the $1-million increase in real property value. The state usually sets a maximum percentage and a maximum length, and the local community has discretion within those limits. Economic development directors who serve multijurisdictional regions will need to know the tax abatement policy and past practice of each of the communities in the region.

Personal property tax. Not every state has a personal property tax, but where it exists it has important implications for economic development. In many industrial plants, personal property values are greater than the value of the factory building. Most states with a personal property tax have a wide variety of exemptions to the tax. Many states, for example, exempt all inventory, goods in process, and raw materials. Certain short-lived tools, dies, jigs, fixtures, molds, patterns and special gauges used in manufacturing may also be exempt from local property taxes. Air and water pollution control facilities that protect the general public from industrial effluent or waste will be exempted from taxes in many states. Although state law governs in such matters, the local assessor may have an influence in borderline situations.

In addition to these complexities, local governments depreciate personal property for tax-base assessment purposes. The depreciation schedule will differ from state to state and from one kind of equipment to another. A firm may also have to pay personal property tax on equipment that it leases. In those states that enable tax abatement, abatement rules apply to personal as well as real property.

The economic development staff should be prepared to communicate to prospective businesses whether its state has personal property tax, what kind of exemptions exist, and what kind of depreciation schedules are used to depreciate personal property.

Local sales and income taxes. Although a sales tax is usually a state tax, some states, such as Colorado, enable local jurisdictions to levy an add-on sales tax. This naturally has implications for retail business, and the economic development coordinator should be prepared to describe the sales tax picture for jurisdictions in his or her region.

Similarly, many states have local income taxes. Actually, local income taxes and local payroll taxes are often lumped together, and a municipality may have either or both. They carry different implications for business, however, and should be understood separately. A city levies a payroll tax against income earned within its jurisdiction no matter who earns it, and levies an income tax against residents of the jurisdiction who earn income. A person who crosses jurisdictional lines while commuting to work may pay one tax to one community and the other tax to another.

Although corporations usually do not pay these taxes, they may effectively pay a part of the tax through a demand for higher wages by taxed employees.

State sales tax. Nearly all states have a sales tax, but one must know more than the tax rate. State sales taxes differ widely in what they tax. The economic development professional must ask: To what degree does a state sales tax cover food purchased for local consumption, and to what extent does it cover services? Sales taxes are designed to tax final sales, not wholesale transactions, but the definition of a "final sale" may vary from place to place. This definition can make a difference in the taxation of industrial activities.

State business taxes. It is not quite accurate to talk about corporate income taxes at the state level. Some states do not have a corporate income tax at all, while others have a business tax that covers a variety of business organizations beyond just the standard for-profit corporation. Michigan, for example, has a "single business tax" that taxes all businesses whose revenues exceed a prescribed level. This includes sole proprietors, partnerships, subchapter S corporations, or any other for-profit business activity.

Unemployment compensation. Unemployment compensation is a nationwide tax administered at the local level. Not only do states differ somewhat in how they administer the program, but the rate may vary from state to state. One way the rate varies is through the penalty tax. If a state's unemployment compensation fund is sufficiently in debt to the federal government, the law requires that a penalty tax be charged to all employers in that state to rejuvenate the state fund.

Research

Although "high-tech" is oversold as an economic development concept, nearly all businesses have a research component. The term "research facilities" refers to anything from a good library to extensive laboratories. As research has become more important to businesses, it has also become more expensive. Even many large firms cannot afford the facilities to do all their research in house. Smaller businesses desperately need to join forces with others to pay for research facilities, or rely more on specialized public and private institutions. Pre-product development, the important stage of product development in which theoretical discoveries are conceptualized as marketable products, has risen out of the financial reach of nearly everyone.

Both to support existing businesses and to attract new ones, the economic development planner should know the research facilities in his or her community. This may include for-profit and nonprofit laboratories, or computer facilities, that are available for hire. It may include university facilities and services. It may also mean knowing what kind of research talent exists in a community.

As the link to the university becomes increasingly important, economic development planners should be acquainted with the university structure and the offerings of any university within a short drive of their town.

Quality of Life

"Quality of life" is difficult to integrate into a local economic development action plan. It is often the miscellaneous category added to any list of business location criteria, but it is clearly an important variable in business location and economic development. Roger Schmenner's survey of U.S. businesses, pertaining to their state and regional plant location choices, revealed that 35 percent of the respondents identified an "attractive place for engineers/managers to live" to be a "must" in their location decisions (Schmenner, 1982, p. 150).

For some firms that are footloose (i.e., not tied either to a source of raw materials or to geographic markets), quality of life may be the most important business location variable. Such firms include research and development operations, and the communications industry. As these industries gain an increasing share of total economic activity, quality of life will increase in importance.

Quality of life is not only difficult to define, but changes over time with changing attitudes. Locational decisions are made by management; therefore the community must appeal to management. When management takes into account the needs of employees, scientists, engineers, and executives are given the greatest weight. While one generation of professionals looks for communities with a good climate, the next seeks communities with progressive values. A decade later the "in" place to live has outstanding social and cultural amenities. Although the early 1970s saw people leaving large metropolitan areas, the emergence of two-professional-breadwinner families caused a return to metropolitan areas. Here, a spouse can find alternative jobs without forcing the entire family to move (Malecki, 1984).

Attempting to make a community desirable for industrial location by chasing lifestyle fads is neither possible nor desirable. Certain local amenities seem to be continually important, however, and some of these are clearly within the control of the local community. Studies of scientists and engineers indicate they prefer areas with a large university nearby, good local schools, and well-maintained public facilities (McElyea, 1984).

Education consistently ranks high among quality-of-life variables affecting industrial location. Executives and professionals concerned for their children place importance on it; it affects the quality of the labor force (see "Labor") and local research and development capacity (see "Research"). Roger Smith, former president of General Motors, indicated that Tennessee's quality of life and focus on education were key factors that tilted the balance in favor of Spring Hill as the site for Saturn Corporation's first automobile plant. "As we looked around, we were thoroughly impressed with Tennessee's commitment to education," said Saturn president William Hoglund (*Detroit Free Press*, August 12, 1985).

The maintenance of public facilities refers to all the physical artifacts owned by the various governmental jurisdictions, but may also indicate a high quality of service resulting from those public buildings and infrastructure. Health care can be a particularly important local service amenity. In at least one case, a major industrial firm located a new plant because the firm's chief executive had an unusual health problem, and the local university hospital specialized in the treatment of that problem.

Although economic development directors can never be sure what quality of life variables will make a difference, they should document the amenities of the community that make it a special place to live and work (see Table 2.2).

PROBLEM IDENTIFICATION:
BUSINESS RETENTION SURVEY

The best way to know whether the community satisfies the needs of local businesses is to ask them, using a business retention survey. Before embarking on a discussion of this concept, however, a preamble is necessary. In most communities, businesspeople are, by nature, very cynical about government and anything government does. They face the cost of taxation every day, and governmental paperwork causes constant annoyance. Cultural differences exist between those who are attracted to the public sector and those attracted to the private sector. Quite probably, where economic development planning is undertaken by the public sector, this cynicism will continue no matter how good a job the economic developer does, and no matter how much local businesses benefit. This does not imply that the job of the economic developer is hopeless or that public-private ventures should not be undertaken. Rather, it is offered as one of the subtle dynamics of the process.

Business retention surveys are commonly used, but vary widely in form. A business retention survey is essentially a questionnaire sent out to existing businesses asking questions about the needs of the firm and how well those needs are being met. The economic developer follows up this mail questionnaire with some personal interviews. When business retention surveys initially became popular, the inclination was to ask too many questions. Partly because of cynicism toward government, many businesses felt that this was a nuisance at best, and an invasion of privacy at worst. Questions related to the firm's wage scale and its projected future growth could be used by competitors, if put in the wrong hands. Successful business retention surveys ask a smaller number of questions and make it clear that the respondent is meant to be the chief beneficiary. Remembering that the purpose of the business retention survey is to promote the success of local businesses, the most successful surveys focus on two open-ended questions: "What single thing would make your business more successful?" and "What single action could this economic development office take that would make your business more successful?"

NEEDS OF THE LOCAL ECONOMY

Because of the importance of economic stability, a community should know what end markets its major employers serve, and how those end markets behave during typical economic cycles. It should also know linkages between local firms. Some firms may sell primarily to one local manufacturer, and are therefore tied indirectly to one outside market. This section provides a simplified description of economic cycles and their impact on local economic development planning.

Throughout much of its history the United States' economy has experienced periodic business cycles. These cycles vary in length, but tend to average approximately four years from peak to peak. Business cycles are caused by fluctuations in interest and inventory levels. As interest rates fall, those economic activities that are highly interest-sensitive experience growth. The residential construction market grows early in the cycle. Since nearly all homes are financed, and since developers rely heavily on financing, the construction industry is interest sensitive. Industries tied to construction, such as lumber and cement, lag slightly behind the construction cycle. Consumer durables turn around next. A combination of increased consumer confidence and lower interest rates allows consumers to buy cars and appliances. Similarly, businesses buy new machinery and equipment during periods of lower interest rates. They are further induced to do so by increased demand for their products.

Figure 2.3
Business Cycle Relationships

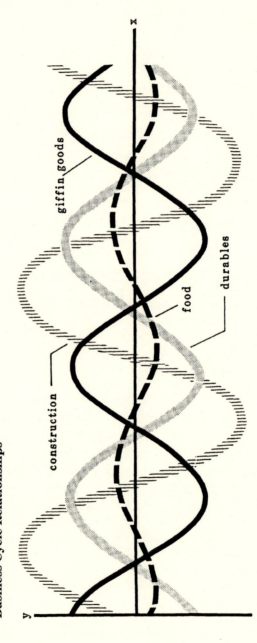

These stimulants cause employment to rise, and increased consumer confidence causes consumer buying to increase. Late in the business cycle, employment is high, buying is heavy, and people begin to use large amounts of installment credit. Businesses take out short-term debt to increase inventory to be prepared to meet increasing demand. The pendulum effect reverses the cycle when demands for credit drive interest rates back up. Construction is the first industry to be adversely affected. Then the decline in employment, coupled with increases in interest rates, cuts into the purchases of durable goods. Finally, confidence and consumer buying decline. Producers of consumer goods are faced with high inventories and the need to cut back on production. The cycle is complete when the reduction in credit demand causes interest rates to decline.

The point to be made here is not just that business cycles work, but that various industries experience their peaks and troughs at different times. If a community wishes to have a broad and stable economic base, it must attract and hold firms that are out of phase with one another. In this way, their overall employment level remains more stable. Downtown stores have a more constant market; local banks avoid cyclical pressures, and the welfare cycle is relieved.

Figure 2.3 shows a simplified model of the relationship between various business cycles.

3

Public-Private Partnerships for Urban Economic Development

INTRODUCTION

"Public-private partnerships" are currently a popular concept. The phrase is used loosely to refer to a variety of activities in which the public sector induces the private sector to behave in desired ways by becoming a partner with it. The methods for carrying out such partnerships are limited only by the imagination, and economic development offices are becoming increasingly innovative in their use of the concept.

The purpose of this chapter is to define and describe public-private partnerships on the assumption that the use of the concept is an important part of any economic development program and is the conceptual link between the economic development information discussed in Chapter 2 and the specific activities delineated in Chapter 4.

The first section in this chapter defines public-private partnerships and gives a brief history of the concept. The second section discusses the economic philosophy that surrounds the use of public-private venture arrangements. The third section discusses organizational structures that make such partnerships legally possible. The fourth section catalogs specific activities and acts as a transition to Chapter 4 on economic development programs.

Background, History, and Definition

Until the 1980s, cities in the United States relied on the federal government for assistance in effecting the development of urban areas. This reliance dates back to the urban programs of the Roosevelt administration's New Deal. It continued with the urban renewal programs of the 1940s, through Lyndon Johnson's Great Society programs of the 1960s, and the community development block grant and revenue-sharing programs of the Nixon era. Funds from these programs were used to clear slums, upgrade the built environment, improve public infrastructure, and create jobs for the city's unemployed.

The 1980s, however, brought a very different order for addressing the revitalization of U.S. cities. Federal budget cuts in the programs most directly affecting urban areas and a change in the global patterns of economic activity mandated that new avenues for urban economic development be explored (Weaver and Dennert, 1987). More specifically, the "New Federalism" of the Reagan administration placed the burden of urban revitalization squarely on the shoulders of the cities themselves (Ledebur, 1984). These local entities became more creative in their search for funds to fill the void created by the federal departure.

In addition to this change in funding pattern, structural changes in the national economy have caused firms to leave the central cities of the older northeastern and midwestern cities. These cities have been left to cope with social and economic problems at the same time that their tax bases have declined. This situation has led city governments to seek to attract private capital and private involvement in the solution of problems that have traditionally been within the virtually exclusive purview of the public sector. This alliance has come to be known as public-private partnership and has become commonplace in most U.S. cities.

Many of the activities that will be described in this chapter have been common for decades. They are outgrowths of the early federal programs previously mentioned. Housing and urban renewal programs, for example, which began in the 1940s, set up nonprofit development corporations to assemble urban land, improve infrastructure, and sell improved property at below cost to private developers. Zoning incentives have also been evolving at least since the 1960s.

The difference starting in the 1980s from the previous three decades lay in the need for local governments to innovate in ways that did not involve the federal government and that therefore required a greater share of private participation. Necessity has been the mother of invention: The current compendium of public-private partnership tools is the result of over four decades of experimentation in the delicate relationship between the public and private sectors within a variety of economic, social, and political ambients.

There have been numerous attempts to define public-private partnerships comprehensively and precisely. They have been called a type of "third-party government." Some have referred to the concept as neo-corporatism (Weaver and Dennert, 1987). Perhaps the most complete definition comes from the Committee for Economic Development:

> Public-private partnership means cooperation among individuals and organizations in the public and private sectors for mutual benefit. Such cooperation has two dimensions: the policy dimension, in which the goals of the community are articulated, and the operational dimension, in which those goals are pursued. The purpose of public-private partnership is to link these dimensions in such a way that the participants contribute to the benefit of the broader community while promoting their own individual or organizational interests. (Holland, 1984)

Due to its nature, the concept lends itself well to the urban planning process in that it brings together the two principal players in urban policy formulation and implementation. Indeed, when the urban planning process carries the label "strategic planning," public-private partnership is considered essential to its success (Sorkin, Ferris, and Hudak, 1986). The fact that the public-private partnership arrangement attempts to balance self-interest with the public interest makes it all the more attractive in a democratic society.

Philosophical Foundations

The concept assumes that a free market system is the most appropriate mechanism for allocating goods and services. It implies that government should leave to the private sector all activities that can be carried out by the private sector. If the private markets do not operate efficiently or do not produce outcomes desired by public policy, the public sector should carefully use both the carrot and the stick to nudge the private sector in the proper direction. The stick represents laws and regulations that coerce individuals and companies to follow some minimum standard of behavior. The carrot represents incentives for more desirable behavior that take the form of either relaxation of regulations or financial inducements. It is the carrot side of the equation that is generally referred to as public-private partnership. The following describes the philosophical foundation of public-private partnerships and provides some conceptual examples that meet the philosophical criteria.

Perfect Competition

Public-private partnerships start with the assumption that the free competitive market is the best allocator of goods, services, and resources in our society. It is the best expression of people's desires, their willingness to pay, and their ability to pay. The phrase "free competitive market" implies, however, a marketplace that meets certain criteria. If it does not meet those criteria, then it is not a good allocator. Economists define a free competitive market as one that experiences perfect competition. Such a market has the following characteristics:

1. A very large number of buyers and sellers participate in the marketplace such that no single buyer or seller has a significant impact on the market.

2. The product sold in the market is highly divisible; that is, it can be purchased in small individual units.

3. Each unit of product is identical in quantity and quality.

4. The price of each unit is based on supply and demand using an auction market methodology.

5. All buyers and all sellers have perfect knowledge about all matters related to the functioning of the market, including price and quality.

6. No externalized costs or benefits result from behavior of the market participants.

A model expresses an ideal state that never completely exists. A good market that properly allocates goods and services is one that approaches the perfect competition model. If a market has a number of serious flaws in comparison with the model, it may not be a good allocator of goods and services. It may in fact cause serious distortions throughout the economy.

Real Estate Markets

When analyzing urban development, one finds that the markets affecting the way cities function and grow are often in a middle ground. They function as private markets, but with numerous imperfections relative to the economist's perfect competition model. Rather than offering a large number of highly divisible homogeneous units, the real estate market is made up of many unique parcels of land, each with its own locational characteristics, shape, size, and infrastructural services. Locational factors can change rapidly as urban infrastructure is added and traffic patterns change.

Typically, market participants' accessibility to knowledge about the market is not good. Dealing in the real estate market involves many secret negotiations, trades, and special prices.

The number of buyers and sellers of each unique parcel is quite small and each seller is nearly a monopolist for that parcel. Externalities abound in the real estate market since the use of one property greatly affects the value of surrounding properties.

Housing Market

Many imperfections are peculiar to the housing sector of the real estate market. Racial and ethnic discrimination causes major imperfections in the operations of the market, for example. Since housing is a necessity, variations in an individual's ability to pay for housing segments the market, and ability to pay is greatly influenced by interest rates that influence finance charges.

Certain segments of the housing market do not work very well. While housing markets are highly localized, it is probably correct to say that no housing problem exists for middle-class Caucasians in North America. Profit margins have been adequate in most cases to induce private builders to supply single-family houses and condominiums at a price affordable to middle-income families. While credit markets are cyclically tight, the system has, in general, provided adequate financing for house purchases.

The housing market for low- and low-middle-income families has not worked very well. Lower-income people face locational constraints that are more severe than others, thus forcing them to compete for a smaller set of units. Transportation disadvantages and the need to be close to services or industrial jobs force lower-income urban residents to look for housing in areas of the central city where land costs are higher and housing stock is older. These factors, when combined with racial discrimination, cause the market rent for low quality apartments to be even higher than for higher quality apartments in suburban areas. The financial intermediary markets for housing also tend to break down in central city neighborhoods available to lower-income families. Banks are reluctant to lend to prospective home buyers in neighborhoods they perceive as at risk of decline, particularly if the loan applicant is already a borderline applicant in terms of financial resources.

A vicious circle of events ensues in which flaws in the market for moderate-cost housing create or exacerbate other flaws. The result is a breakdown in the ability of the free market to adequately supply housing to certain segments of the population.

Resulting Externalities

Similar problems can be traced through other segments of the real estate market. Because of the high level of externalities associated with real estate development, a district's social, economic, and physical trends may be difficult to alter. Developers might be reluctant, for example, to create a high quality mixed-use development on a waterfront, even if the demand for waterfront development is high. If the waterfront is currently occupied by declining industrial plants, railroad yards, and docks and is inaccessible by modern transportation, externalities will overpower market forces.

Common externalities associated with aging communities may include the following:

1. Antiquated subdivision of land, as characterized by irrational lot lines, resulting in odd-shaped or small plots that impede parcel assemblage for development.

2. An aging infrastructure that is expensive to repair and/or replace, yet discourages economic development when left untended. Due to fiscal problems, many older central cities have adopted programs of deferred maintenance for their public infrastructure, which serve only to exacerbate the problem.

3. The mixing of incompatible uses of land, which ultimately blights the affected area and reduces property values. This situation reduces property tax revenues generated by the area, which in turn diminishes the city's ability to provide public services. Thus a vicious circle is created.

4. Social disorganization, which reduces the quality of life in a given urban area and may ultimately disrupt commerce.

5. A poorly educated and trained workforce, which is unattractive to new high-technology industries, thereby diminishing the given area's potential for renewal.

6. Environmental contamination with accompanying cost and liability.

Any one of these factors, and certainly all of them together, can make a particular urban area difficult and prohibitively expensive to revitalize.

Justification for Government Involvement

Because of the existence of market imperfections, it is sometimes necessary for governments to intervene. Few would question that assertion, although the degree and level of intervention are matters of debate.

The real question concerns the method of intervention. One approach is for government to take over a market and provide the goods or services directly. This is an appropriate solution where market imperfections are overwhelming and permanent, where the product is indivisible, economies of scale are large, externalities are enormous, information is bad or impossible, and the market becomes monopolistic. National defense is the ultimate example of such a "product." The temporary government takeover of a market might be reasonable in order to establish and stabilize markets that have been severely affected by external events. The direct provision of housing to a nation torn by war or earthquakes is an example.

A second approach is for government to act to perfect the markets. If market imperfections are causing severe dislocations, thereby inducing private businesses to behave in ways that are contrary to public policy, one approach is to see how the characteristics of that particular market deviate from the model of perfect competition. Government should then act to bring the behavior of the market closer to that of the model.

ORGANIZATIONAL STRUCTURE OF PUBLIC-PRIVATE PARTNERSHIPS

Public-private partnerships are not just organizational structures, but processes to achieve public and private objectives. These strategic collaborations take on several forms and are useful urban revitalization tools in a variety of circumstances. They are sometimes created to address a single development issue or carry out a single project. In other cases, they stand as permanent associations prepared to address ongoing issues within their jurisdictions (Hamlin and Lyons, 1996).

To develop an understanding of public-private partnerships, it is useful to explore the forms these processes take, their legal structure, primary sources of funding, and leadership arrangements. Some may be completely equal partnerships between government and business, while others are largely private organizations with public officials serving on their boards of directors (Levy, 1981). Funding for these activities may come from private sources, public sources, membership fees, income earned from development, or from other partnerships (Ahlbrandt and Weaver, 1987). The following section is a further examination of the various structures used to facilitate public-private partnerships in the United States and other parts of the world (Hamlin and Lyons, 1996).

Mixed Partnerships

A partnership is "a voluntary contract between two or more competent persons to place their money, effects, labor, and skill, or some or all of them, in lawful commerce or business, with the understanding that there shall be a proportional sharing of the profits and losses between them" (Black, 1968). In a legal sense, "persons" include legal organizational entities such as corporations or other partnerships and individual citizens. This legal arrangement has been extrapolated to similar arrangements between public and private organizations. Public organizations such as cities are legally nonprofit corporations and can enter into partnership arrangements. Some intersectoral partnerships are simply legal arrangements in which both the government and private participants maintain their autonomy. They agree to work cooperatively to solve local problems for the benefit of all parties. The contributions of the parties to such a collaboration need not be equal (Hamlin and Lyons, 1996).

The public sector, the private sector, and other nonprofit organizations may form either single-purpose or multipurpose mixed partnerships. That is, one mixed partnership may deal solely with marketing or promoting the community. Another may engage in planning, research, and community development (Ahlbrandt and Weaver, 1987; Hamlin and Lyons, 1996).

United States tax law affords certain advantages to a partnership. Paper losses resulting from declaring real estate depreciation expenses pass through to the partner's tax return, offsetting other real estate profits. Partner liability constitutes the disadvantage of a partnership structure. Liability is not limited as it is with a corporate structure (Hamlin and Lyons, 1996).

Limited Partnerships

In a limited partnership one or more of the legal individuals act as general partners, while the remaining participants act as special (limited) partners. These special partners contribute funds but are not liable for the debts of the partnership beyond this contribution. The general partners manage the funds, select sites, and carry out the actual development effort (Thomsett, 1988). For example, the government and a private business may form a limited partnership for the redevelopment of a particular area in the city. The government and the private business are the general partners in this limited partnership. They then sell limited partnership units (shares) to investors who seek an adequate return on investment (Hamlin and Lyons, 1996).

If the project can be structured to provide an adequate return on investment, the general partners provide leadership and the limited partners provide equity financing with limited risk. For the general partners the tax advantages and liability disadvantages of a straight partnership pertain (Hamlin and Lyons, 1996).

Mix Condominiums

Under a condominium arrangement, individuals own distinct physical parts of the development project. As members of an association they also own other parts of the project in common. The most typical condominium is a multifamily housing complex. Here, members of the association own the interior walls and fixtures of each housing unit privately, while exterior walls, facilities, and grounds are owned in common. Voting power on association matters is often allocated by unit. Alternatively, it can be based on the number of square feet owned, the value of each unit, or other factors (Hamlin and Lyons, 1996).

A condominium may have commercial, office, industrial, or residential uses. An interesting arrangement is where governmental or quasi-governmental entities own some private units. One example is when an industrial park is organized as a condominium with a government as the owner-developer. This arrangement allows for lot lines to move to fit the needs of the incoming companies without the legal problems associated with replatting.

Another project has an office tower, hotel, parking garage, and recreational plaza. The condominium consists of three separate ownership units plus areas owned in common between the three. The three units are the hotel, owned by a national franchise; the office tower, owned by a real estate development firm; and an underground parking garage, owned by the city. The common areas consist of the land, the foundation, the plaza, and an atrium between the tower and the hotel. The three unit owners contribute equally to the cost of maintenance of the atrium and superstructure and have equal vote in the association. Because of the size of each ownership unit, the authors call this a mega-condominium (Hamlin and Lyons, 1996).

A condominium within a condominium is also possible. One group of units may own some property in common, and this group, as a whole, may be a unit in a larger mega-condominium arrangement. This allows for mixed uses in a legal condo arrangement in a planned unit development (Hamlin and Lyons, 1996).

Governmental Authorities

Semipublic organizations created by government statute or ordinance are typically governmental authorities. While some are publicly financed, they function independently of state and local government. Port authorities, transit authorities, and economic development corporations number among their ranks. They possess some of the flexibility of a private corporation while maintaining some of the powers of public entities (Levy, 1981). This is especially useful for generating central city development (Hamlin and Lyons, 1996).

Port and Transit Authorities

While their primary function is to provide for security, maintenance, and traffic control at seaports, many port authorities have staff that specialize in promoting and facilitating development within their local areas (Conway, 1966). Port authorities promote their facilities to industry (Gilmore, 1960), provide information on potential plant locations in their areas, and supply data on tariff rates, transportation schedules, and engineering considerations (Conway, 1966). Some port authorities plan industrial districts and additional port facilities within their jurisdiction (Gilmore, 1960; Hamlin and Lyons, 1996).

Transit authorities participate actively in local development, but less so than port authorities. Their development efforts include promoting their jurisdictions to industry and cooperating with businesses in providing service. They offer ridership data to businesses seeking to assess the availability of local labor, or the local market for their products and services (Lyons, 1987; Hamlin and Lyons, 1996).

State Level Development Corporations

In the United States, many states have created development authorities. Included among these organizations are the New Hampshire Community Development Finance Authority (http://www.nhcdfa.org/); the Illinois Development Finance Authority (http://www.graphicsdept. com/~gdi/idfa/programs.htm); the Indiana Development Finance Authority (http://muncie.com/finance_auth.asp); the Arkansas Development Finance Authority (http://www.ark.org/adfa/chair_ltr.html); the Washington State Development Finance Authority (http://www.owt. com/tri-cities/business/wedfa.html); the Wisconsin Housing & Economic Development Authority (http://www.wheda.com/about/aboutwheda. stm); the Nevada Development Authority (http://www.nevadadevelop ment.org/about.cfm); the New Jersey Development Authority (http:// www.njeda.com/); the Kentucky Development Finance Authority; the Pennsylvania Industrial Development Authority (Sharp, 1983); and the Michigan Economic Development Corporation. These authorities encourage development by making mortgage insurance and loans available to private firms to assist them in purchasing land, buildings, and capital equipment (Sharp, 1983). They also operate capital access pro-

grams and micro loan programs, provide export financing, and offer
energy and environmental loan guarantees, to name a few. Some offer
more comprehensive development services such as job training, employee recruitment, and site preparation.

Some states have more than one semiautonomous development corporation. New York has several. One of the oldest of these state-level
development authorities is the New York Job Development Authority (d/b/a Empire State Development Corporation). State seed money
helped to launch this public purpose corporation in the 1960s. It is now
funded through the sale of state-backed bonds to various institutions
and individuals and has become completely self-supporting. An eleven-
member board directs the Job Development Authority. The board consists of the State Industrial Commissioner, the State Commissioner of
Commerce, and the State Superintendent of Banking (all ex-officio
members), and seven members appointed by the governor with the approval of the state senate (Sharp, 1983, p. 30; New York's Public Authorities, 2000).

Local Economic Development Corporations

Sometimes called community development corporations or industrial
development corporations, local economic development corporations
(EDCs) are also semipublic local development authorities. The public
sector creates and partially finances them (Gilmore, 1960). They also
raise money by selling stocks and bonds, issuing notes, or soliciting
contributions (Gilmore, 1960). They are semipublic because their purpose is to generate community economic development, not to realize a
profit. Because they have a strong private affiliation, they are often
more effective in dealing with prospective firms than the local government is. Economic Development Corporations help manufacturing
firms by rehabilitating abandoned factories or constructing new ones
and leasing this space to them. They also make loans to businesses for
constructing new plants, purchasing land or equipment, paying relocation costs, and so on (Gilmore, 1960; Hamlin and Lyons, 1996).

A primary activity of local economic corporations in the United States
has been the floating of private purpose tax exempt bonds (see "Tax-
exempt Bonds") (Hamlin and Lyons, 1996).

Downtown Development Authorities (DDA)

A downtown development authority is an organizational technology
created to help revitalize declining downtowns. DDAs are excellent ex-

amples of organizations devised to carry out public-private partnerships. State enabling law and local ordinance often give powers that allow them to act as both small governments and private companies in appropriate situations. They resemble little municipalities. They have a jurisdictional boundary and a governing board made up of owners of homes, businesses, or real property within that jurisdiction. In many states they have taxation power and can float tax-exempt municipal bonds. They also might play the role of a tax increment finance authority (see TIF section). One of their most common activities is to improve the public infrastructure in their jurisdictional area (Hamlin and Lyons, 1996).

They also have the power to invest in businesses, lend to firms, build and own real estate, and earn a surplus from successful business ventures. In this way they are more like economic development corporations (Hamlin and Lyons, 1996).

Other Local Development Authorities

A variety of specialized local development authorities have formed in recent years to promote economic development. Brownfield redevelopment authorities have become common and utilize many of the powers of the other authorities already mentioned. This may include the ability to float tax-exempt revenue bonds, and buy, improve, and sell land. At least one state enabling law allows the local brownfield redevelopment authority to establish a baseline environmental assessment and property value for ad valorum tax purposes. It then institutes a tax increment financing (TIF) procedure to support the floating of a bond, whose revenues are used to clean up and rehabilitate brownfield lands. The tax revenues resulting from the increment in land value are then used to pay off the bonds. (see TIF section) (Hula, 1999).

The increased use of conditional land transfers for economic development have also created new kinds of local economic development authority. Conditional land transfers are an effort to ease annexation fights around the United States over economic development projects. Suppose a major industrial development wants to acquire expanded space on the fringe of a city. Rather than fight over whether the land must be annexed into the city to receive urban services, the central city and the surrounding suburban jurisdiction set up a cooperative agreement whereby both the city and suburb receive some of the tax revenues and are responsible for some of the services. The zone may be transferred conditionally to the city and they may then set up a joint authority to oversee it. The authority may then be given powers to float bonds, engage in tax increment financing, offer tax abatements, and enter into partnership arrangements with the private company to ensure that the development project is successful.

Private Corporations with a Public Purpose

Nonprofit Corporations

A nonprofit corporation in the United States can be either a stockholder or a membership organization. It may be formed to carry out a limited set of activities that are deemed to be for the public good. Because of the public benefit from these activities, the corporation may be granted nonprofit status at each of three levels (Hamlin and Lyons, 1996).

First, the state that charters it will designate it as a nonprofit if its articles of incorporation and by-laws produce an appropriate organizational structure and scope of activity to meet state law. Second, the U.S. Internal Revenue Service may grant the corporation tax-exempt status if it meets their criteria. The most coveted IRS designation is 501(c)3. With this designation, any surplus revenues are tax exempt and donations by private individuals to the corporation are often tax-deductible donations Third, the local government may independently determine its exemption from local taxes such as property, income, and sales (Hamlin and Lyons, 1996).

Stockholders of nonprofits cannot make a profit off their stock, and nonprofits are, in general, restricted from competing with for-profits. Nonprofits can engage in a wide variety of business activity such as making loans and investments, buying and rehabilitating real estate, and entering into partnerships with other individuals and businesses. Nonprofits can also form for-profit subsidiaries or enter into joint ventures that can engage in any legal business as long as the subsidiary pays taxes on its profits before distributing dividends back to the founding nonprofit organization. Foundations, municipalities, and community development organizations are all examples of nonprofit organizations that may engage in community economic development (Hamlin and Lyons, 1996).

Because donations to tax-exempt organizations are often tax deductible, nonprofits can generate substantial corporate equity. They accept donations from wealthy for-profit corporations and individuals attempting to avoid income and inheritance taxes. This equity may then be used to leverage other private investments. Such organizations can, for example, form a joint venture with a for-profit organization such that cash surpluses are funneled to the nonprofit and all tax advantages are given to the taxpaying corporation, providing maximum benefit to both. The equity of the joint venture can then be used to attract limited partnership equity or debt capital. Once the project is under way, the nonprofit corporation can recycle its earnings into other activities (Hamlin and Lyons, 1996).

It is often beneficial for land to be owned by nonprofits and leased to a desirable private development. Land is not depreciable, so this arrangement concentrates the tax benefits of depreciating a project in the for-profit entity but keeps ultimate control of the land in the hands of the nonprofit.

For-Profit Corporations with a Public Purpose

Any corporation may be established to carry out a public purpose. Its articles of incorporation might require that the board of directors be structured to represent a cross section of the community and may restrict the activities in which it may engage. The founders may have reasons why they do not want to pursue nonprofit status. A local certified development corporation is an example of such an organization in the United States. A certified development corporation may be organized as a for-profit, but in order to receive U.S. Small Business Administration certification, its board of directors must broadly represent the diverse interests of the community and it must refrain from certain for-profit activities. The primary purpose for its existence is to act as a conduit for federally guaranteed, second position small business real estate loans. A Business and Industrial Development Corporation (see BIDCO later in this chapter) is also typically a for-profit corporation with a public purpose (Hamlin and Lyons, 1996).

The best example of a private for-profit corporation with a public purpose is found at the national level in the United States. It is the Federal National Mortgage Association (FNMA or Fannie Mae). Originally established as a federal government corporation, FNMA became a private corporation in 1968. With stock traded on the New York Stock Exchange, it has 30,000 stockholders (Flick, 1987). Its connection to the government is maintained through the five members of its board of directors appointed by the President of the United States (Flick, 1987). Fannie Mae operates under a mortgage-backed security program. It buys loans, repackages them into securities, and sells these to private investors (Flick, 1987; Hamlin and Lyons, 1996).

ACTIVITIES OF PUBLIC-PRIVATE PARTNERSHIPS

A purpose in establishing collaborative arrangements for urban revitalization that cross sectoral boundaries is to influence development in a specified area. This purpose assumes that the community recognizes that problems or opportunities exist in the designated area (Fosler and Berger, 1982). The benefits brought to such a partnership by the public sector include the legal, political, and large-scale service-provision advantages not available to the private sector, working alone. For its part, the private sector brings the needed investment in labor, capital, and know-how sought by the government. This relationship is each entity carrying out the tasks for which it was created in harmonious concert for mutual, and ideally community-wide, benefit. In this respect, cross-sectoral alliances represent democratic and capitalistic principles in their purest form (Hamlin and Lyons, 1996).

Key to the establishment of these partnerships is local initiative, which includes "strong civic foundations" and capable leadership (Fosler and Berger, 1982). The elements of a strong civic foundation include: community-wide concern; openness to public participation in the decision-making process; community vision; awareness of local strengths and weaknesses; effective civic groups; networking among community leaders; a nurturing environment for "civic entrepreneurs"; and continuity and flexibility in policy (Fosler and Berger, 1982; Sorkin, Ferris, and Hudak, 1986). A civic foundation with these characteristics will tend to spawn the kind of leadership necessary to create public-private partnerships for urban revitalization (Hamlin and Lyons, 1996).

The leader(s) may come from either sector, and rarely come from both. In most cases, one sector takes the lead and the other assumes the role of facilitator (Fosler and Berger, 1982). The same rules apply when third sector entities are among the partners. Once the partnership process is in place, leaders must focus on the activities that will enable it to achieve its established goals (Hamlin and Lyons, 1996).

The following section is a more detailed discussion of these public development-inducing activities. The organization of this section follows a standard outline of the needs of a business firm. This format was chosen because it is private firm behavior that the public sector is attempting to influence. The relevant categories used are: land and related capital, labor, energy, finance, management, taxes, and research. Within this outline, subcategories of activities are described. The final subsection talks about focusing and integrating all other activities in a single project area (Hamlin and Lyons, 1996).

Land and Related Capital

Land Location, Acquisition, and Assembly Assistance

As discussed previously, the marketplace for urban land suffers several imperfections. In older areas experiencing urban decline, externalities related to land are particularly problematic. The public sector in most countries can use its special powers to assist private developers in overcoming some of the problems related to their need for land so as to promote economic development and urban redevelopment (Hamlin and Lyons, 1996).

In its simplest form, one approach is to help locate suitable parcels for the type of development being sought by a business. This serves to reduce the time and effort a private developer must put into site location research. Aided by the increased use of geographic information system (GIS) technologies, many cities maintain a computerized inventory of available vacant land within their jurisdictions. This provides site-specific information on zoning, acreage, street location, assessed value, and terrain and other development constraints (Carlson and Duffy, 1985). This type of assistance makes the urban area that offers it considerably more attractive to private investors due to reduced opportunity cost alone. This service is not only for outsiders looking to come into a region, but also for existing business wanting to expand (Hamlin and Lyons, 1996).

Local governments may seek to assist private developers in acquiring land so as to reduce the cost of development. A private developer typically must assemble several parcels of urban land to have enough space for a modern development. In older areas of a city, chaotic subdivision of land, as characterized by irrational lot lines, resulting in odd-shaped or small plots impede parcel assemblage for development. Because some landowners may resist selling until afforded a higher price when they learn that their parcel is essential for a new development project, the process of assembling land may become cumbersome, slow, and exorbitantly expensive. Government can help by using its power of eminent domain to buy and assemble parcels for a large development project and then sell them to a private developer. One can argue that this intervention by government into the real estate market does not distort the market but rather perfects it by making real estate more liquid and more functional (Hamlin and Lyons, 1996).

Landbanking

In some countries, land in deteriorating areas becomes very inexpensive due to urban decline and problems with irregular parcels. Some landowners in arrears on taxes may abandon their property rather than pay. In other cases, government may acquire property in order to tear down vacant buildings blighting the community. Instead of reselling this property at the depressed price, many cities hold on to ownership, creating a "landbank." This land is then accumulated until parcels are large enough to facilitate significant modern development. Landbanking deals with more than unused vacant land. Useable structures can be leased during the accumulation period (Blakely, 1994) or land made available for parks, playgrounds, and community gardens (Hamlin and Lyons, 1996).

Land Improvements

Physical improvements to the land refer to the improvements in a city's infrastructure (NASDA, CUED, and the Urban Institute, 1983). Infrastructure, broadly defined, is "the set of those life-support and public facility systems which must be provided in order to enable the development of healthy human settlements" (Dajani, 1978). Infrastructure systems in urban areas include roads, public transit, schools, water treatment facilities, street lighting, transmission lines, sewer facilities, parks, and other recreational facilities, (Dajani, 1978; Juergensmeyer, 1985; Levy, 1988; Hamlin and Lyons, 1996).

While most infrastructure is clearly in the public domain, its quality is crucial to the success of private development, thus creating an important point of intersectoral collaboration. Government can have a significant effect on development simply by consciously targeting its limited infrastructure resources toward high-priority locations such as new industrial parks or redevelopment areas (Hamlin and Lyons, 1996).

Excess Condemnation

Excess condemnation is taking, by right of eminent domain, more property than necessary for the creation of a public improvement and, after completing the project, selling or leasing this excess. On the theory that the value of the excess lands will have increased by virtue of their proximity to the improvement, it is held to be within the power of government to sell these lands at an increased value to some appropriate user. In other words, the local government makes a profit on the sale of land surrounding the public improvement and uses this profit to help pay for the improvement (Hamlin and Lyons, 1996).

Some argue that this practice puts government in the real estate speculation business. Others argue that the government project caused the surrounding land to increase in value, not action taken by private owners. If government does not use excess condemnation, then private landowners experience speculative gains in wealth without having added any value to society to justify those gains. Furthermore, a major public project may induce rapid development of surrounding land that may not be its long-term highest and best use. The resulting development pattern may, in fact, diminish the usefulness of the original public improvement. The clogging of expressway interchanges is an example. For these reasons, U.S. courts have upheld excess condemnation as a legitimate exercise of government powers (Steiss, 1975; Hamlin and Lyons, 1996).

An example of effective use of excess condemnation is where a local government, planning to build a new airport, condemns more land than is necessary to accommodate the airport. Then, after leaving enough room for future airport expansion, it develops an air industrial park surrounding the airport, selling the prime industrial land for more than the original condemnation price (Hamlin and Lyons, 1996).

Land Readjustment

Through negotiation between property owners, land readjustment redraws property lines in a given redevelopment area so as to produce more rational and functional parcels of land and allow for the modernization of infrastructure. This is done with a minimum amount of property transactions or the use of condemnation. To the extent possible, land ownership remains in the hands of the original owners in approximately the same proportion and location as before the readjustment (Hamlin and Lyons, 1996).

Government has an important role in this process as an intermediary agent between property owners. In the right urban circumstances, property owners would be anxious to engage in this process since the parcels of property that would result would be more valuable on the real estate market and more usable for modern development. Government would most likely be one of the property owners, as the owner of rights-of-way and public facilities (Hamlin and Lyons, 1996).

Land readjustment is most effective where (1) location affords high development potential, but (2) antiquated parcel sizes and shapes and antiquated rights-of-way retard that development potential, and (3) existing above ground improvements have low value relative to the potential value of the land. In short, land readjustment is useful where historic ownership patterns are keeping land from being put into its highest and best use. A prime candidate for this activity could be an antiquated and deteriorated district on the fringe of a prosperous CBD. It might also prove valuable in the development of an industrial park in an urban fringe area that previously experienced poor subdivision control (Hamlin and Lyons, 1996).

Japan has used land readjustment extensively. Cultural factors and high land values make land readjustment an important alternative redevelopment method and the Japanese Land Readjustment Law is one of the major tools of public-private partnership and urban renewal in that country. The cultural importance of family land ownership makes the purchase or condemnation of land difficult there (Hamlin and Lyons, 1996).

The Japanese development profession has used land readjustment for a wide array of development endeavors including inner city redevelopment, fringe development, and new towns. The Land Readjustment Law is more complex than the simple description provided above. Under the system a development agency (often Urban Development Corporation of Japan [JUDC]) defines a project area. It then works with the property owners inside the project area to create a future development plan. Property owners may be home owners, store owners, industrial corporations, railroads, governmental agencies, or any other legal entity (Hamlin and Lyons, 1996).

As part of the implementation of the plan, property lines are redrawn to create parcels that are more conducive to real estate development and the construction of modern infrastructure. Small parcel owners, such as a house owner, may need to be compensated for their parcel with cash or some ownership in the final development project such as a condominium unit. In all cases owners are given an option that constitutes a real estate trade so as to avoid a legal sale that would invoke the payment of capital gains taxes. Because of rapidly rising land values in the postwar era, capital gains taxes can be a severe penalty for participation in a redevelopment project and fear of capital gains taxation has retarded or constrained redevelopment. As a result, the "trade" provision is an important inducement to cooperation with a land readjustment project (Hamlin and Lyons, 1989; Hamlin and Lyons, 1996).

Once property lines are readjusted, JUDC begins physical implementation of the project plan through the construction of modern infrastructure. An example is widened and realigned roads. The JUDC might also construct multiple-use utility tunnels through which telephone, electrical, and water lines may run (Hamlin and Lyons, 1989; Hamlin and Lyons, 1996). After infrastructure modernization, landowners may develop their land in general accordance with the project plan that has been agreed on and sanctioned by law. Public landowners may develop parks, community centers, or other public uses that enhance the overall development and further induce the private owners to build according to the plan. Private developers may sell or lease their land to JUDC, which then earns a surplus by developing the site. They could also hire JUDC to build and manage a project owned by the land owner (Hamlin and Lyons, 1989; Hamlin and Lyons, 1996).

A common feature of land readjustment is that each existing landowner is typically offered a slightly smaller parcel after readjustment than she or he initially held. This contribution by each landowner, often as much as 35 percent, is primarily to provide the additional space needed by modern infrastructure such as wider streets. Despite the reduction in ownership area, the individual's holding should be significantly higher in value than before readjustment. A more rational shape to the parcel, and the improved infrastructure, greatly increase its development potential (Hamlin and Lyons, 1996).

Often the aggregate amount of land contributed is more than necessary for infrastructure. The excess is consolidated through the redrafting of boundaries into one large parcel. A quasi-governmental corporation such as the Urban Development Corporation of Japan (JUDC), a New York Urban Development Corporation-type organization, takes ownership of the resultant parcel. This contribution is payment to JUDC for its coordination function and its investment in infrastructure. The parcel becomes a "profit" sector that JUDC can then sell, lease, or develop to generate revenues to pay for its contribution to the project. This process functions as a kind of voluntary excess condemnation (Hamlin and Lyons, 1996).

The book *Land Readjustment: The Japanese System* provides a thorough examination of the land readjustment policy in Japan (Minerbi et al., 1986). The study's purpose was to offer policy makers in Hawaii a basis with which to judge the appropriateness of this development tool to their situation. Hawaii faces similar development problems to those of the Japanese, given the island's location and limited development area (Hamlin and Lyons, 1996).

Germany, Australia, South Korea, and Taiwan also use this technique (Schnidman, 1988). Most of these countries have engaged in land readjustment projects for many years (Schnidman, 1988). Recently, communities in the United States have tried activities similar to land readjustment, carrying such names as commercial development pooling, negotiated replatting, and residential neighborhood pooling (Schnidman, 1988). Oregon, for example, uses negotiated replatting to modernize "antiquated subdivisions" in rural areas (Nelson and Recht, 1988). Land readjustment was first used in the United States in 1791, when George Washington employed it to implement Pierre L'Enfant's plan for Washington, D.C. (Schnidman, 1988). Although current U.S. approaches to land readjustment are "watered down" relative to the system in other countries, they provide examples of the melding of land assembly and public-private partnership activities to achieve local economic development (Hamlin and Lyons, 1996).

James L. Northrup (1986) tells the story of Dallas' use of what he calls an "assemblage partnership" to revitalize that city's Farmers Market district. It is home to a large municipal produce market covering approximately 100 acres. Landowners in the district, including the Southern Pacific Railroad, the city, and a number of warehousing operations, were concerned about declining land values and the general deterioration of this downtown fringe area. The private landowners in this group formed a partnership that served as the single owner of their combined properties. Additional investors were attracted to purchase other privately held parcels. All told, the private partnership gained control of over 45 acres in the district, and the city controlled 47 acres of its own. Recognizing the mutual benefit to be gained from working together, the private partnership and the city entered into their own partnership for the redevelopment of the area by negotiating property exchanges and cost-sharing agreements for needed public improvements (Hamlin and Lyons, 1996).

The partnership then negotiated with James Rouse's Enterprise Development Company to build a festival marketplace in the district to act as an anchor for leveraging further development. The private partners realized substantial profits by selling off their assembled parcel to a development syndicate, which carried the project forward with the Enterprise Development Company. The city gained an attractive, well-planned, and economically viable addition to its central business district and the resultant property tax revenues (Hamlin and Lyons, 1996).

While U.S. examples represent a weaker version of land readjustment than found in other countries, the potential for applying the model to the U.S. situation in the foreseeable future is strong. States such as California, Hawaii, and Florida have studied the adoption of land readjustment enabling legislation (Schnidman, 1988; Hamlin and Lyons, 1996).

Land Write-Downs

A land write-down occurs when a government or quasi-governmental agency sells land to a private business for less than the market price. The public sector may have acquired the land originally through eminent domain as a part of a land assembly program or confiscated it for taxes in arrears and may have held it in the city's land bank. City governments frequently use this inducement to encourage development of parcels in the central city that might otherwise remain vacant or underdeveloped. Significant infrastructure improvements and boundary readjustments are often made before sale. Sometimes the land is sold for $1.00 or given away if the developer agrees to develop it in accordance with the city's plan (Hamlin and Lyons, 1996).

Nonprofit Ownership and Leaseback

Key to public-private partnership success is creating a situation where the private sector can earn an adequate return on investment while developing or improving a declining or difficult part of the community. In real estate, depreciating the property so as to reduce private income tax burdens is an important part of the equation. Yet land cannot be depreciated. One method for improving the private developer's return-on-investment calculation is for a nonprofit corporation to own the land and lease it, long term, to the development project. This reduces the upfront capital required by the private developer and offers the developer more concentrated tax benefits from depreciation of the improvements. In other words, it increases the dollar of tax benefit per dollar of initial investment. It also keeps control of the land in the hands of a nonprofit organization with the community's long-term vision for the area.

Land Use Control Incentives

Although zoning regulations and other land use controls have been viewed by many in recent years to stand as barriers to development, this planning tool was originally created as a means of protecting property values and encouraging investment in the late nineteenth and early twentieth centuries. After the phenomenal growth of urban areas in the 1950s and 1960s, zoning was used by many local governments in the United States to slow and redirect growth, making it appear to be anti-growth. Today, localities use land use controls as an incentive to private investment. Some examples are described below.

Incentive zoning has been a popular approach to encouraging development in America's large cities, while at the same time promoting open space, landscaping, public art, and other cultural amenities. Most incentive zoning permits developers to build higher (more floors than the base zoning ordinance allows) in exchange for the provision of a public plaza, or other amenities, on the site. An example of successful incentive zoning is Chicago's First National Plaza. The developer built a large terraced plaza, with an attractive display of public art and a staging area for outdoor entertainment in the summer, in exchange for the right to add several stories to the First National Bank Tower on the same site. Developers have responded well to the opportunity to build at higher densities. In New York City, incentive zoning has been so successful in developing portions of Manhattan that the city has had to eliminate this incentive in those areas to prevent overbuilding (Hamlin and Lyons, 1996).

Performance zoning can also be used as an inducement to development. It allows for the location of uses that may be considered incompatible adjacent to each other, provided they are carefully sited and properly screened. The standards that must be met by these adjacent land uses are quantified, and therefore less subjective than those of traditional zoning ordinances. Private developers find that their costs are often reduced by performance zoning because of its greater flexibility with regard to land use and the benefits derived from the clustering of development, which this technique encourages (Hamlin and Lyons, 1996).

Mixed use developments (MXDs). The separation of land uses through land use controls has been more strictly applied in the United States than in most other countries, sometimes to the detriment of innovative development. As the term implies, mixed use development allows for multiple uses on a single site, usually including retail, office, residential, and recreational uses. Developers like the additional markets that are opened to them by such an arrangement and the reduction in risk that a multiple use development affords. Among other advantages, built-in markets for retail activities are created. MXDs make sense from a planning perspective as well, in that they encourage internal and pedestrian traffic in the central city, as opposed to automobile traffic coming in from the outside (Hamlin and Lyons, 1996).

Air Rights and Transfer of Development Rights

Many cities have adopted a policy of selling "air rights" to private developers to induce central city investment. The concept of air rights dates back to common law, wherein fee simple ownership of land included not only the real property at ground level but the space extending below the parcel to the center of the earth and above it to the sky (Donohoe, 1988; Hamlin and Lyons, 1996).

Much of the land located in central cities is owned by the government, including public buildings, parking structures, highways, parks, and sports facilities. Most of these public facilities do not make full use of their air rights, nor is it likely they will be doing so in the future. Some enterprising cities are selling these air rights to private developers who are permitted to use them to increase the intensity of development in targeted renewal areas (Hamlin and Lyons, 1996). Private development might be built over a public facility. An example would be an office complex constructed above a public parking lot or a submerged urban expressway. In other cases the rights are transferred to another parcel as a transfer of development rights. The parcel of land receiving the additional development rights may be adjacent to, or on the same block as, the land from which the rights are being sold. In still other cases, development rights may be transferred greater distances (Schlefer, 1984). The city generates revenue from this sale to reinvest in public infrastructure or the provision of other public services, and the developer obtains the right to build at greater densities than local ordinances might otherwise permit (Hamlin and Lyons, 1996).

Transfer of development rights also has been used as a way of concentrating development in selected areas while preserving open space, farm land, or low-density development in other areas. The governmental entity will pass an ordinance that creates a sending zone and a receiving zone. The private property owners in the sending zone are then able to sell development rights to private property owners in the receiving zone who use them similarly to the method described in the previous paragraph. As a result, senders or sellers receive a financial incentive to preserve the current character of their area while receivers or buyers gain the right to develop their property more intensely (Machemer, 1999).

Labor

Structural Unemployment

As mechanization continues to replace manual labor in nearly every part of the world, the skills, talents, and attitudes of the local labor force become more critical. An important alliance between the public goals of the community and private success focuses on education and training of the workforce (Hamlin and Lyons, 1996). Time and talent are perishable resources, so not utilizing the labor force to its fullest is a terrible loss to the individual, the community, and the economy. Structural unemployment and underemployment refer to the subset of individuals who are not employed or not fully utilizing their abilities because of a mismatch between the skills in demand in a given location and the skills available. Because of the locational facet of structural employment, communities and individuals can be big winners if they partner with business to reduce structural unemployment (Hamlin and Lyons, 1996).

Labor Force Training

Local governments in the United States and elsewhere have become involved in training and retraining local workforces. This is not surprising given the dramatic economic restructuring that has gone on. With the decline in traditional heavy industry and the rise of high-tech businesses, an appropriately skilled labor pool is a very valuable resource to a city seeking to attract development. A study reported in *Area Development* magazine found that the "availability of skilled labor" was third on the list of the top twenty site selection factors from 1989 to 1993, and was increasing in importance (Laughlin and Taft, 1995). If a locality can successfully anticipate the demand for skilled labor by the private sector and meet that demand, it can gain an advantage in the market for new development (Lyons, 1987). Several methods the public sector uses to provide skilled labor as an inducement to private urban development are described below (Hamlin and Lyons, 1996).

Recruiting and screening. Nearly all state governments in the United States provide the service of recruiting and screening employees for firms operating in their state. The state's employment security division, or its counterpart, normally offers this service. The local offices in cities throughout the state maintain regularly updated, computerized data banks on job opportunities and labor pool availability. Participating firms receive a list of qualified applicants for each advertised job opening, using this data and an interview process. This service saves firms time and money (Hamlin and Lyons, 1996).

Industrial training. Industrial training programs are a more proactive nonfinancial incentive often provided by the public sector. The majority of these job training programs are "customized" to prepare workers for employment in specific industries, or individual businesses, that are the focus of public sector planning efforts (NASDA, CUED, and the Urban Institute, 1983). Government can, in this way, select the firms it wishes to encourage to invest in the local community by affording specialized training. Public universities or community colleges in the area often develop these programs. They sometimes offer them at the business site or through distance learning technology including salellite TV and the internet. The cost of the program is typically shared through some combination of the business, the state and local governments, the institution of higher education involved, and maybe labor unions.

Retraining. Government retraining programs seek to lure investment by certain firms by providing a more appropriately skilled workforce. This service has been very important in recent years in the heavy manufacturing states of the northeastern and midwestern United States. These areas have suffered through numerous manufacturing plant closings and "downsizing" activities, leaving thousands of persons without jobs and without the necessary skills to obtain new ones. By retraining these individuals, the public sector helps to reduce unemployment while establishing an attractive labor pool (Hamlin and Lyons, 1996).

Employability training. Training must be perceived broadly. Despite current trends toward training as a solution to structural unemployment problems, job specific training, while important, is best described as the necessary icing on the cake. Occupational training cannot be utilized by the individual until a large number of other kinds of skills are acquired. To take advantage of training programs, an individual must have sufficient capacities in language and computational skills. A large percentage of individuals with labor market problems do not have satisfactory competence in basic skills. Also, an individual must be prepared to cope psychologically and socially with the labor market. No level of training or other assistance will enable an individual to obtain and maintain work if this prerequisite is not met. The coping concept refers to several personal attributes. Central to coping is a positive self-concept. If a person has a positive self image, he or she is in a better position to relate well with fellow employees and supervisors, be self-motivated, and have a positive attitude about work. Self-concept development also creates assertiveness in less assertive individuals and enables one to be realistic about one's own career aspirations. A sound self-concept is imperative for an individual to deal emotionally with periods of cyclical unemployment and avoid problems of health and home relations that may transform cyclical problems into chronic physical, economic, and social disorders. (Muth, Hamlin, and Stuhmer 1979; Hamlin and Lyons, 1996).

Energy

One need only consider the effects of the oil shocks of the 1970s or the price spike in the year 2000 on the world economy to appreciate the importance of readily available and relatively inexpensive energy to successful local economic development. When a major source of energy becomes scarce and expensive at any location at any point in time industries that rely on it are adversely affected. Firms may find they must reduce their production or relocate if adequate and reliable supplies of reasonably priced energy are not available at their current locations (Hamlin and Lyons, 1996).

Two important considerations that must be addressed by local economic development planners are: (1) the reliable supply of relevant types of energy for local users and (2) the cost of this energy. As the Rocky Mountain Institute points out, 80 to 90 cents out of every dollar spent for energy is permanently lost to the local community (Browning and Lovins, 1989; Hamlin and Lyons, 1996).

Ensuring sufficient, reliable, and affordable energy may not be easy in the future. World demand is accelerating as newly emerging economies become more affluent, and the supply line is less stable. World environmental pressures such as global warming might also affect future energy availability and mix (Mintzer et al., 1996). Ensuring local supply entails several activities: (1) securing the reliability of existing sources, (2) conserving existing nonrenewable sources, (3) effectively using renewable sources, and (4) developing totally new energy alternatives. Because the energy industry is replete with public and private organizational types, an understanding of intersectoral partnerships is crucial to all these activities. Nonrenewable sources of energy are oil, natural gas, and other fossil fuels (Hamlin and Lyons, 1996). Renewable energy consists of five categories: hydroelectric power, geothermal energy, biomass, solar energy, and wind energy (Michaels, 2000).

Ensuring the reliability of local energy requires working closely with local utilities to spot problems of grid overload or failure that might develop in the future. Sharing planning information on local population and economic projections is part of that process. Promoting a mix of energy types and sources might also help. The Public Utility Regulator Policies Act of 1978 continues in 2000 to require that alternative sources of power must be purchased and/or wheeled over existing utility grids. Furthermore, competition between power providers is now being implemented in many local areas.

Numerous techniques have been used for conserving nonrenewable sources. Weatherizing buildings in cold weather climates is one approach to conservation. Local governments can partner with local utilities to save energy dollars by underwriting the cost of aerial and ground level infrared analysis. Heat-sensitive film picks up points of heat loss in buildings. When these photographs are shared with local firms and home owners, they are able to target portions of their buildings that are in need of weatherization. This is a relatively inexpensive way to foster good public-private relations and conserve fossil fuels. Distribution of information instructing residents and businesses on conservation techniques may also have a big payoff (Hamlin and Lyons, 1996).

Some publicly and privately owned utilities engage in a variety of programs to conserve energy and use renewable resources. Some have established co-generation plants, which reuse waste heat. This not only saves renewable energy sources, cutting waste energy of a power plant by 30 to 70 percent (Alliant, 2000), but may attract business because it constitutes a new energy resource (Browning and Lovins, 1989). Alliant Energy of Madison, Wisconsin, for example, receives power from a central Iowa wind farm, the methane extracted from a landfill, a used tire burning plant, and a small dam, and is working with a hospital to build a geothermal facility (Alliant, 2000).

Offering financial incentives to firms that adopt conservation strategies is another approach to energy conservation. Legislation at the state level is helpful in this endeavor. Nearly all states have some incentive programs and most have several. Incentives include tax breaks, special grants, loan programs, and loan guarantees to businesses. States also provide incentives to local governments to induce them to set up revolving loan funds and other programs geared to energy conservation, alternative energy production, or new energy sources. States also provide some incentives to utilities to pursue a greater variety of energy options. Arizona, for example, offers corporate and personal tax deductions and credits for alternative fuels use as well as solar and wind system purchases. The state also has a revolving energy systems loan program and works with utilities on their solar partners program and remote (off grid) residential solar electrical system lease/purchase program. Iowa offers local option special assessments for wind energy devices, ethanol-based fuel exemptions, wind energy equipment sales tax exemptions, state grants for energy efficiency and renewable energy, the state Energy Bank loan program, and the Renewable Fuels Fund. In all, eleven states have personal energy income tax breaks, eight states offer corporate tax breaks, sixteen states allow property tax exemptions, and nine have sales tax exemptions for energy equipment. Eight have small grants for alternative energy projects, twelve states have loan or loan insurance programs, and eleven have partnering programs (North Carolina Solar Center, 2000).

Greater use of solar, wind, geothermal, and hydroelectric energy can both increase and diversify the local energy supply. For example, numerous localities have adopted ordinances that permit, with some restrictions, wind energy conversion devices (windmills) within city limits. Wind farms, fields full of windmills whose power is harnessed to generate electricity, are now found throughout the world (Browning and Lovins, 1989). At present, commercial wind farms can be found in California, Hawaii, Massachusetts, Montana, New Hampshire, New York, Oregon, Vermont, and Wyoming, to name a few (Browning and Lovins, 1989; Hamlin and Lyons, 1996).

Small dams may be a source of energy and income for a community. Approximately 50,000 small dams (defined as less than 100 feet in height) exist in the United States. Many of these currently produce some energy, and another large portion did generate power but were abandoned in the 1960s when energy seemed cheap. The current level of energy costs, however, has again made electricity production feasible at such dams. This feasibility, combined with the emergence of some new technologies, such as the bulb turbine, has increased the viability of small hydro as a salient energy source (Clarke et al., 1979). Through a combination of public and private initiatives these dams can be rehabilitated and retrofitted to produce a low cost and reliable source of energy for the community's economic base. The retrofit process also produces jobs, and the area surrounding the dam can be an attractive and unusual green space and recreation area for local residents (Hamlin and Lyons, 1996).

One example of a retrofitted dam is on the Huron River near Belleville, Michigan. In the 1980s Van Buren Township worked with the Trade Union Leadership Council of Michigan to retrofit the small dam for hydroelectric generation and build a fish ladder while employing and training disadvantaged youth from Detroit to prepare them for entry into the building trades. This dam continued to generate electricity in the year 2000. Belleville Lake and the area surrounding the dam are also important community amenities (Hamlin and Lyons, 1996).

The importance of energy to state and local economic development has become widely recognized. Local and state governments are partnering with the private sector to ensure that ample, affordable energy is available to keep local economies functioning (Hamlin and Lyons, 1996).

Finance

Financial intermediaries are at the center of the economic development process, acting as the bridge between the critical functions of savings and investment. An alliance between public purpose and private purpose has always been critical to the intermediary process. Yet seldom do intermediaries exist in enough variety to serve diverse economic needs. The process particularly breaks down in underdeveloped regions or areas of decline such as low-income urban neighborhoods (Hamlin and Lyons, 1996).

Understanding how to skillfully lubricate the financial intermediary system can benefit the local community in two ways: (1) by attracting investment capital to the area and (2) by inducing developers, industrialists, and other businesses to put that capital to work in ways that promote public goals. On the saver side of the equation, the secret is the ratio of risk to reward. One must either reduce the risk of putting savings into the desired investment vehicle or increase the reward. On the side of the business borrower, the intention is to make investment capital easier to acquire by making it more readily available and reducing its cost. Several types of incentives may be employed to accomplish these goals. Some examples are described in the next section (Hamlin and Lyons, 1996).

Loan Guarantees

Loan guarantees afford the backing of loans made by private lending institutions. If the recipient of the loan defaults, the government steps in to cover part, or all, of the losses. With this protection, private lenders experience less risk; thus they are more likely to lend to small businesses, other higher-risk firms, or businesses in at-risk neighborhoods. They might also lower their interest rates (NASDA, CUED, and the Urban Institute, 1983; Hamlin and Lyons, 1996). The backing for the loan may be the "full faith and credit" of the government or some other dependable quasi-public asset. "Full faith and credit" commits future tax revenues of the government to covering bad loans. Other assets include revolving loan fund balances or other dependable revenue streams.

If carefully implemented so that no loans experience problems, this method costs the government nothing. However, since the purpose of a loan guarantee program is to increase capital flow to higher risk situations, loan guarantees are likely to cause some losses to taxpayers. By involving the private sector, the cost should be far less than if government acted alone. In this case, loan guarantees represent a kind of indirect subsidy to both lenders and borrowers for the sake of promoting public policy. It is a partnership in which all parties share in the risks and rewards (Hamlin and Lyons, 1996).

Since the issue is how best to balance risks and rewards for both lender and borrower so as to induce desired economic activity, deciding the amount of the guarantee and the amount of the down payment is important. Decreasing the percentage of the loan that is guaranteed puts more of the risk on the lending institution, and increasing the down payment causes the borrower to be at greater risk (Hamlin and Lyons, 1996). Where possible, employing loan guarantees to promote public policy is preferable to lending money directly since this approach maximizes use of existing private financial intermediary institutions and minimizes the impact on the natural marketplace. A difficult challenge is designing rules that focus investment on accomplishing public goals while opening the process sufficiently to provide a fair opportunity for all potential borrowers and lenders (Hamlin and Lyons, 1996).

Loan Insurance

Private insurance companies also back loans, providing the same kind of lender risk reduction as governmental guarantees. The insurance companies are selective in the loans they will guarantee, preferring very large loans so as to reduce processing and oversight costs. They charge a premium to cover their risk and provide a return on investment. This premium greatly increases the cost of the loan to the borrower. One alternative is for local government to subsidize the loan insurance premium for those business ventures that clearly benefit targeted disadvantaged areas or otherwise promote public policy. In this way the public interest is pursued at minimal cost using private investment systems (Hamlin and Lyons, 1996).

Loan Insurance Fund (LIF) or Risk Pooling Program

A loan insurance fund or risk pooling program is a reserve fund established to insure future losses from a portfolio of loans that banking institutions make under the LIF program. If a business that requests a bank loan is considered to be too risky for conventional bank financing, the owners may be offered participation in the LIF. They are then requested to pay an additional fee equal to a fixed percent of the loan amount into the insurance pool. If any of the participating loans become nonperforming, the pool may be used to cover the bank's loses after collateral recovery. This additional protection allows banks to stretch their risk tolerance when these "almost bankable" businesses are willing to pay an extra fee into the pool. By carefully managing the risk associated with the portfolio of all participating loans vis-à-vis the size of the pool, the bank spreads the risk and allows a broader spectrum of businesses to receive financing than otherwise would.

While the concept sounds plausible in theory, few banks have begun such a program on their own. Perhaps they have felt businesses would not pay the additional fee necessary to cover the risk, or bank regulators have not been sufficiently convinced of the backing provided by the common loan loss pool. In 1987, the state of Michigan began a program called the Capital Access Program (CAP). Since then twenty-two other states and two cities have successfully adopted similar programs (Hamlin, 1999). This program, which is described fully in Chapter 4, provides government sanction for the loan loss insurance pool concept and offers just enough state sharing of the risk to cause large numbers of banks and borrowers to participate.

BIDCO Financing

A business and industrial development corporation (BIDCO) is another arrangement to plug the medium-risk gap. The level of risk/reward with which BIDCOs deal is in fact slightly higher than that for LIF programs.

Commercial banks are the primary source of debt capital in most communities, and a loan insurance pool can extend somewhat the level of risk banks can take. Yet, because the primary source of bank funds is deposits from the public, banks must be highly regulated institutions, focusing on the low-risk, low-return end of the business financing market (Williams, 1986). The savings and loan debacle of the 1980s illustrates dramatically what happens when the risk/reward and regulatory environments become unbalanced at depository institutions (Hamlin and Lyons, 1996).

BIDCOs have been created to be "nonbank" lending institutions designed to serve business financing needs with risk/reward levels beyond those served by commercial banks, even with loan insurance funds. The BIDCO's source of capital is private investor equity, or the purchase of stock, not individual deposits, as in banks. As a result, government can provide a more relaxed regulatory environment to BIDCOs than that faced by banks. In addition, the public sector often furnishes these companies with below market rate debt and matching equity funding. With this combination of resources and regulatory flexibility, BIDCOs make loans to small businesses unable to acquire traditional bank financing. These loans are at higher rates than bank loans, and BIDCOs can demand inclusion of an equity kicker (see the equity kicker section in this chapter) not allowed to banks. The state of California established BIDCO financing in 1977, and other states, including Michigan, adapted the California law to their situation (Hamlin and Lyons, 1996).

Micro Loan Program

This unusual form of financial intermediary draws investment funds toward small start-up businesses. This is a niche that few other sources will touch because of the high risk and high service cost. Yet financing this sector is important to diversify the local economy and provide opportunities for individuals with good ideas but few traditional credentials or contacts to put their skills and imagination to work. The program starts when a group of banks agrees to make a loan to the micro loan pool. The program structure minimizes the risk to the bank. The funds are lent to a broad spectrum of business and the program uses peer pressure strategies and risk pooling to ensure repayment. These features will be described below. In the United States, banks are often willing to be involved because of the community service requirements of the Community Reinvestment Act (CRA). The amount of the initial pool might be augmented with a donation from a local benefactor or a foundation, thereby decreasing the bank's risk still further. The local governmental body or a revolving loan fund of one of the quasi-governmental organizations might also participate in the initial loan to the pool (Hamlin and Lyons, 1996).

The second step is for a program administrator to invite a limited number of micro businesses to participate. A micro business is typically three or fewer employees. Peer groups of approximately five businesses are formed. The peer group simultaneously serves as a social support group, a peer pressure group, and a financial risk cushion (Hamlin and Lyons, 1996). In the beginning each participant is allowed to take out only a very small loan, perhaps $1,000, from the micro loan pool established by the initial bank loan. Often all members of the peer group must co-sign each other's loans. The peer group meets regularly to assess progress and offer mutual personal and business support. Under the rules used by some micro loan programs, if one member of the group cannot make its weekly payment, it must be paid by the others. When one participant successfully pays off a loan on schedule, he or she may graduate to a higher level line of credit. Ultimately, as businesses grow, the peer group breaks up and participants begin dealing directly with the bank or other more traditional sources of credit (Hamlin and Lyons, 1996).

Micro loan programs are often better considered as a part of a larger micro enterprise development program that includes training and other services. This concept is described in greater detail in the next chapter.

Revenue Bonds

Another way for the public sector to attract and channel investment capital is to use its governmental powers to act as an intermediary. Often a governmental authority can promote the securitization of projects by acting as the issuer of revenue bonds and then lending money to the project from the proceeds. Typically this is done through a quasi-governmental corporation such as an economic development corporation or an industrial development authority and is called a private purpose revenue bond. In such cases, the government experiences no direct legal risk because the bond buyers are dependent on the success of the project for repayment of the bond. Failure of the project causing a default on the bond does not endanger the general fund of the community. Unfortunately, since the revenue bond is sold by the municipality, its financial reputation may be harmed (Hamlin and Lyons, 1996).

Usually, enabling law requires demonstration of a public purpose before government may exercise this intermediary function. An example would be a redevelopment project in a declining area. The interest on these bonds may be either taxable or tax exempt, as described below (Hamlin and Lyons, 1996).

Tax-Exempt Revenue Bonds

Tax-exempt bonds, as the name implies, are bonds that can be sold by the local government at a lower rate of interest because interest accrued is exempt from income taxation—this means federal taxes in the United States and the state's income taxes in the state where issued. This amounts to an indirect interest subsidy, or low-interest loan, from the exempting government via the intermediary local government to the bond seller (NASDA, CUED, and the Urban Institute, 1983). The method is not as effective in countries where income taxes are less important or where the effectiveness of tax collection is poor (Hamlin and Lyons, 1996).

Tax-exempt revenue bonds must be sold through a public body such as a municipality or a state government in order to maintain their tax-exempt status. Usually the proceeds must be used for a public purpose, but often this public purpose can promote private real estate development. An example is the use of special assessment revenue bonds to build the infrastructure needed by a project. In this way, the developer pays the city for needed infrastructure, but uses tax-exempt financing through the special assessment process. Another example occurs when municipal revenue bond financing is used to build a parking structure that is important for a major private development project. Use of the structure must generate revenues to pay off the bonds, either by charging a user fee or renting part or all of the structure to the adjacent development project (Hamlin and Lyons, 1996).

A variety of private purpose tax-exempt bonds exist in the United States, the most common of which is the industrial revenue bond (IRB). In the early 1980s, prior to 1987 changes in U.S. income tax laws, IRBs were the most popular type of financial incentive for economic development (NASDA, CUED, and the Urban Institute, 1983). The projects allowed under IRB programs have included industrial buildings, warehouses, industrial parks, medical facilities, certain recreation facilities, and pollution control systems (*Site Selection Handbook*, 1985). The tax reforms previously mentioned, which went into effect in 1987, eliminated commercial IRBs and approximately one-half of all these bond issues for industrial purposes (Hamlin and Lyons, 1996).

Revenue Bond Insurance

Because revenue bonds are paid off through the success of a particular project, they are sometimes perceived as risky and illiquid, forcing the interest rate up. For large projects, bond insurance is sometimes purchased from a company specializing in this activity. If the entire value of the bond is insured in this way, the rating on the bond may be that of the insuring company. The insurance premium is generally high, forcing up the cost of the loan to the borrower. The public sector may subsidize this insurance for projects it deems particularly important or may insure the bond itself using quasi-public funds such as the balance on a revolving loan fund (see below). Saline, Michigan, for example, used the revenue stream from a tax increment financing district (described later), which included a new industrial park, to insure revenue bonds used to develop the industrial park and sell parcels to private firms (Hamlin and Lyons, 1996).

Revolving Loan Funds

Local governments or their financial authorities sometimes make loans directly to private investors. In this way, the government assumes the role normally fulfilled by a commercial lending institution such as a bank. However, this should be a last resort and government should only become involved if private lenders will not. Governments usually avoid competing directly with banks (Hamlin and Lyons, 1996).

Interest rates on these loans may or may not be below market rate.

In many cases these loans may be payable over a longer term than loans available from private lenders. The greatest advantage afforded by these loans is their availability to firms or investors that, due to their small size or the speculative nature of their operations, are unable to obtain capital from private lending institutions (NASDA, CUED, and the Urban Institute, 1983; Hamlin and Lyons, 1996). The public sector typically places certain conditions on direct loans to ensure that the investment they induce is focused on the public interest.

Revolving loan funds represent one means for administering direct loan programs (NASDA, CUED, and the Urban Institute, 1983). Public and private monies are often used to establish revolving loan funds. When a loan is made from this fund, the borrower pays the principal back into the fund so that it is regularly replenished. Interest on the loan and processing fees are frequently used to cover the costs of administering the fund (Hamlin and Lyons, 1996).

Subordinated Debentures

Generally a debenture is a certificate signed by a public officer of a corporation as evidence of a debt. It is a bond backed by the general credit of a corporation rather than a particular asset. Debentures are purchased by investors or banks. A government or governmental authority could lend money to a local corporation as an incentive by buying debentures from it (Hamlin and Lyons, 1996).

A subordinated debenture is a debt instrument that is subordinated to other specified indebtedness of the borrowing company. In the event of dissolution, subordinated debt comes after these other debt instruments when receiving payouts. As such it is more risky to the lender, the investor buying the debenture, and may be difficult to sell to private investors. By purchasing debentures that are subordinated to a predetermined amount of bank loans, a governmental authority may be able to inject money into a company without diminishing the project's chances of receiving additional bank financing. This is because the bank's loan would have a superior position (Hamlin and Lyons, 1996).

Depository Selectivity

Local governments occasionally have excess cash in their possession. They receive tax payments and other sources of revenues on an irregular basis and must hold it until expenses are incurred or debt payments come due. Local governments, for example, tend to collect property taxes twice a year, while making payment on expenditures all year long. One financial interface between the public sector and the private sector is when government deposits cash reserves for temporary safekeeping. At any point in time, these reserves may be very large, dwarfing the deposits received from other depositors. They may, therefore, have a significant influence on the operation of the financial intermediary system (Hamlin and Lyons, 1996).

Government deposits in banks are like very short-term loans to those institutions. As such, governments should make a conscious choice as to where to put funds in the same way they would scrutinize the making of any direct loan. Safety of the deposit is a primary consideration. Return on investment is another, but the interest earned on very short-term investments will not vary widely between instruments of comparable risk (Hamlin and Lyons, 1996).

One approach to cash management that a government may espouse is to temper its return-on-investment criterion for selecting money market vehicles with an understanding of the potential impact of these cash management decisions on other policy issues. An example of this would be when a local government makes a decision on which bank will receive its cash deposit based in part on which bank is most cooperative in promoting local economic development. In other words, if the Fourth National Bank uses its deposits to make loans to the local community, while Bigger Bank and Trust just deposits its funds in a larger money center bank, then the city government might be more inclined to deposit its excess short-term funds in Fourth National Bank (Hamlin and Lyons, 1996).

Second Position Loan

A second position loan is a subordinate position to another loan using the same real estate development as collateral. Assume, for example, that a mortgage loan is given to help finance a project worth $50,000,000 and the loan is for 80 percent of the project cost. Then a second mortgage is given by a second source for the remaining 20 percent or $10,000,000. In the case of default, the project would be sold and the proceeds would be used to first pay off the original mortgage. Remaining sale proceeds would then be used to pay off the second or subordinated position loan, to the extent possible. The second position loan clearly involves more risk and therefore commands a higher rate of interest. If a government or quasi-governmental authority is willing to make a second position loan for 50 percent of the project cost, developers would have less difficulty finding private financing for the remaining 50 percent since the private financing would have a senior position. In this way the public sector induces private financial institutions to become involved in projects in renewal areas that they otherwise might not (Hamlin and Lyons, 1996).

Buying Loans in a Secondary Market

Buying loans in a secondary market is yet another way to reduce the cost and increase the supply of debt capital. In the primary market, commercial lending institutions make mortgage loans at market interest rates. The secondary mortgage market is where outstanding loans are traded when lenders need funds before their loans are completely amortized (Ammer and Ammer, 1984). By selling these loans to other financial intermediaries in the secondary mortgage market local banks free up funds to make new loans locally. To be marketable in the secondary market, mortgages typically must be written according to a standard "boiler plate." In this way they can be "bundled" with similar mortgages and sold in large denominations. Sometimes investors buy bonds on national bond markets that are backed by the debt service from these bundles. This describes a chain of events in which investors nationally buy bonds, thus allowing secondary mortgage institutions to buy bundles of mortgages, which enables local lenders to make more loans.

Three major secondary mortgage market institutions operate in the United States: the Federal National Mortgage Association (FNMA or Fannie Mae), the Government National Mortgage Association (GNMA or Ginnie Mae), and the Federal Home Loan Mortgage Corporation (FHLMC or Freddie Mac) (Flick, 1987). The first is a private corporation with a public purpose, while GNMA and FHLMC are government corporations. Fannie Mae and Ginnie Mae purchase VA and FHA loans; Freddie Mac has developed a secondary market for loans without VA or FHA insurance (Flick, 1987). The "Big Three," as they are sometimes called, continue to be an important source of mortgage money in the United States (Flick, 1987). The secondary mortgage market should be distinguished from the primary market, where mortgages originate (Jones and Grebler, 1961; Hamlin and Lyons, 1996).

Equity Injections and Equity Kickers

Equity is a private firm's assets in excess of its liabilities. In the case of a corporation, that portion of equity that is owned by the holders of the firm's stock, both common and preferred, is known as corporate equity (Ammer and Ammer, 1984). One way for the public to induce a firm to develop in a particular geographic area or in a particular way is for government to purchase ownership shares of the corporation. Government must be cautious about becoming involved in this type of transaction. It must prove that private corporate ownership is for the health, safety, and welfare of the general public and that it does not adversely impact the rights of other shareholders of either this firm or competing firms. This type of incentive is typically used to induce developers to build in declining areas of the city where they would not otherwise become involved (Hamlin and Lyons, 1996).

In the appropriate situation, injecting equity into a company or a project through the purchase of stock or participation can be a more effective mechanism for inducing development than providing debt capital. Although facilitating loans to a project, or a company, can provide needed capital to promote development, it can also make the company's balance sheet less attractive by increasing its debt-to-equity ratio. This hurts its ability to receive additional financing from private sources. The injection of equity capital, on the other hand, improves the debt-to-equity ratio and increases the project's chances of private financing. In this way a small amount of government equity participation can leverage a large amount of private capital injection (Hamlin and Lyons, 1996).

Viewing the situation in the opposite way, providing a comprehensive package of debt capital and cost reduction incentives to a firm can be expensive for the taxpayer. If the company succeeds, partially as a result of the incentive package, it may be appropriate for the public sector to participate financially in that success. The community will, of course, benefit from the jobs and tax base that result from the firm's success, but the government of the community may want to participate more directly through part ownership of the firm. They may require, in exchange for the incentive package, that the firm gives them an "equity kicker" or part ownership in the business (Hamlin and Lyons, 1996).

Equity financing can take several forms. The following section describes each type of equity financing and how a government might directly participate.

Common stock. This form is a security that represents ownership of a share in a corporation. Common stockholders usually have a direct say in matters concerning corporate operations through a vote at the annual shareholders' meetings, but nonvoting shares are also possible. Owners of common stock bear more risk than either preferred stockholders or bondholders (see below) because they are the last to be paid should the corporation cease operations. On the other hand, common stockholders stand to realize greater payoffs in capital appreciation and dividends (Ammer and Ammer, 1984). The government can encourage private investment by purchasing shares of common stock in private corporations whose activities it wants to influence or promote (Hamlin and Lyons, 1996).

Local public ownership of businesses was historically rare but is becoming increasingly common. Some municipalities are maintaining part or total ownership. Local development corporations in the United States are learning the process of negotiating equity kickers and stimulating venture capital and, as a result, end up in ownership positions (Hamlin and Lyons, 1996).

Multiple classes of common stock. Common stock can be organized into multiple classes (class A, class B, etc.). While all common stock is equally subordinate to all senior securities, each class may have its own set of rights and privileges. Often, equity injections by public or quasi-public sources or equity kickers purchase stock in a separate class from other investors. This separate class may be nonvoting, for example, or may elect a nonvoting representative to the board of directors. In this way it is easier for the public entity to extricate itself from the corporation's business after the public policy goal has been accomplished (Hamlin and Lyons, 1996).

Preferred stock. Preferred stock is also a security, or written document, representing ownership in a corporation, but is senior to common stock (Ammer and Ammer, 1984). This means that should the corporation be forced to go out of business, preferred stockholders would be the first shareholders to be paid from remaining assets. This reduces risk to the preferred shareholder. Dividend rates for preferred stockholders are normally established by the corporation's board of directors and paid ahead of dividends for common stockholders (Ammer and Ammer, 1984). Dividends are more fixed and resemble more closely the interest on debt. In some cases, quasi-public entities purchase preferred stock as an incentive for the appropriate development of a private corporation. In this way, the public sector increases its leverage of private investment capital because of the more positive effect of equity on the balance sheet while sustaining less risk than if it purchased common stock. Government also maintains a low profile in corporate decisions by not having a voting interest (Hamlin and Lyons, 1996).

There are several types of preferred stock that treat dividend payments in different ways. A governmental or quasi-governmental entity will choose from among these depending on how it wants to participate in the project. (See Ammer and Ammer, 1984, p. 361, or Lyons and Hamlin, 1991, p. 99, for more details.)

The existence of public-private partnerships has induced a new kind of preferred stock to emerge. The governmental or quasi-governmental organization using equity injections usually is concerned only with inducing development. It has no desire to maintain long-term ownership in the company. Therefore, it may buy preferred stock with an agreement that the company buy the stock back over time. Since the preferred stock pays a regular dividend, and since the periodic repurchase is built into the deal, the security behaves, from the government's point of view, as if it were a loan. From the perspective of the private firm, it provides the equity advantages to the balance sheet discussed earlier in this section. Normally, nonparticipating, noncumulative preferred stock is used (Hamlin and Lyons, 1996).

Convertible securities. Convertible preferred stock has the characteristics of preferred stock described above but also allows the stockholder to exchange it for a specified number of shares of common stock. This type of preferred stock carries a higher risk than other preferred stock because its price is based in part on the price of common stock. If the company, or this particular development, is highly successful, the convertible clause will cause the price of the preferred stock to rise, following the price of the common stock (Hamlin and Lyons, 1996).

Convertible bonds are arguably another form of equity capital. Much like convertible preferred stock, the bondholder is permitted to exchange bonds for common stock at a specified time and price (Ammer and Ammer, 1984). While these bonds are technically a form of debt capital, the convertibility provision causes the price of the bond to be partly based on the price of the common stock, increasing both the risk and the reward. When an investing government elects to purchase convertible debt, it is, in essence, agreeing to risk greater loss of value for the opportunity to realize a greater return on investment (NASDA, CUED, and the Urban Institute, 1983). The convertibility provision of convertible securities creates a kind of equity kicker (Hamlin and Lyons, 1996).

Royalty agreements. Royalty agreements operate similarly to stock, except that the holder receives as repayment a fixed percentage of the profits realized through the sale of the given firm's product(s). There is usually a maximum royalty. The advantage of royalty agreements is that the government receives a fixed repayment, while the private firm enjoys increased pliancy in the timing and amount of payments (NASDA, CUED, and the Urban Institute, 1983; Hamlin and Lyons, 1996).

Warrants. Warrants are contracts that permit the holder, at its option, to buy a fixed number of shares in a given private firm at a fixed price for a limited period of time. They operate much like a call option. Public and quasi-public lenders often accept warrants as an equity kicker attached to a loan deal. If the shares' value surpasses the price established in the warrant during its term, the public warrant holder can exercise its option to buy shares at the fixed price. It then either holds the shares and continues to participate in ownership or sells them and receives a capital gain. In return, the public sector lender often gives good terms on debt financing to the firm in question (NASDA, CUED, and the Urban Institute, 1983; Hamlin and Lyons, 1996).

Limited partnership units and preference units. If a project is organized as a limited partnership as described in the section on organizational structures, the local development authority can inject equity into the project by purchasing some of the outstanding units. As a limited partner the authority would receive a share of profits. *Limited partnership preference units* give the limited partner first preference over general partners in the payment of any profits. There may also be a limit on the payout that goes to limited partners. This kind of equity instrument behaves much like preferred stock in the way that profits are distributed and risk is experienced, except that the payout qualifies for the same tax advantages as other limited partnership profits. Investors who desire real estate income to offset paper losses from other real estate investments might be interested in the high yield generally offered by these investments (Hamlin and Lyons, 1996).

Indirect Equity Injections

For government to purchase equities directly is sometimes awkward. Often governments act to induce other organizations to provide equity capital. An example of this approach is the Small Business Investment Corporation (SBIC) program, in which the U.S. government gives favorable term loans to specially constituted corporations if they agree to make venture capital investments with that money. These SBICs can be for-profit or nonprofit and typically purchase a controlling interest in a new small business or technology. If the technology succeeds, the SBIC sells its share at a substantial profit, perhaps up to 200 percent gain in three years. These proceeds are used to pay off the government loan and reinvest in other ventures (Hamlin and Lyons, 1996).

Some public entities have used a small portion of a government employer pension pool as a venture capital fund. The state of Michigan, for example, allows for up to 5 percent of the state employees pension fund to be diverted into a venture capital pool. Since pension funds are often large, a small percentage of the fund can create an enormous venture capital pool. The Michigan Venture Capital Program attempts to use its capital to leverage other private venture capitalists to participate so as to minimize the pension fund's own risk exposure (Hamlin and Lyons, 1996).

Pre-venture capital is another financing need that is often difficult to find. Pre-venture capital finances research and development at the product development stage, where new scientific discoveries are translated into marketable products. Without adequate pre-venture capital, many high-tech products would never make it out of the laboratory. Pre-venture capitalists do not buy stock in or control of companies so much as they buy securities that allow them to participate in product success such as patents, product development rights, and warrants. Pre-venture investments are smaller than venture capital investments but are even more risky. Also, since the investment comes at an early stage of product development, pre-venture capitalists need to be more patient. Foundations and the development funds of public and private universities are supplying pre-venture capital, either directly or by partnering with venture capital firms. Some universities have become involved because they are looking for ways to spin off new products developed in their laboratories. They often want to place new companies in university-sponsored research and industrial parks (Hamlin and Lyons, 1996).

Direct Subsidies

Local and state governments, or private foundations, will offer direct subsidies to private firms to encourage their investment in a renewal area. A direct subsidy is a grant of money made to a private entity, without provision for repayment. In most cases such subsidies are tied to efforts by the government to *leverage* private investment in the area targeted for redevelopment. Economic leveraging, like the word from which it is derived, means making large-scale private investment happen with a minimal initial, or "seed," investment by the public sector (Hamlin and Lyons, 1996).

Direct subsidies for urban revitalization generally come in two forms: government grants and private foundation grants. These grants are made with the intent of influencing firm behavior with regard to investment in new and existing facilities within the renewal area. It is hoped that this direct investment will spur further private investment as revitalization begins to take place. There are several ways that this kind of activity can be leveraged and we offer two examples as illustrations. (Hamlin and Lyons, 1996).

The first example pertains to the rehabilitation of low-income housing units in city neighborhoods nationwide. An organization known as the Local Initiatives Support Corporation (LISC) makes grants and low-interest loans to community development organizations for the rehabilitation of housing units for low- and moderate-income families. LISC was originally funded by a grant from the Ford Foundation, which it has used to leverage backing from major corporations, government agencies, and other foundations. The grants and loans made by LISC are used to leverage further investment in a specific project, or an entire neighborhood, by private lending institutions (Cook, 1987).

Among LISC's successes are the rehabilitation of eighty-five apartment units in New York City's blighted South Bronx neighborhood and the construction of 183 units of housing for moderate-income families in the Hough area of Cleveland (Cook, 1987). Often these successes will beget further redevelopment, as visual blight is eliminated and private investors' images of the area change for the better (Hamlin and Lyons, 1996).

The other example comes from Indianapolis, Indiana, where that city has been successful in leveraging central city redevelopment through improvement of the local quality of life. For many years Indianapolis suffered with the image of a nondescript, if not undesirable, city. It was mocked as "Naptown" and "Indiana no place." During the 1970s, the city lost 45,000 residents and thousands of jobs (Bamberger and Parham, 1984). Indianapolis needed a strategy to counteract this decline and elected to depart from traditional economic development approaches to accomplish this. The city hit upon the idea of becoming a sports capital and using the notoriety and prestige generated by this activity to leverage further development (Hamlin and Lyons, 1996).

The first sports facility built was Market Square Arena, a basketball and hockey facility completed in 1974. It was constructed using general revenue-sharing funds (Bamberger and Parham, 1984). Now, as an aging facility, it has been replaced by the palatial Conseco Fieldhouse, and the Arena will be torn down (Sword, 2000). Ten years after the construction of Market Square Arena, the Hoosierdome, a 61,000-seat indoor football facility, was completed. It was funded through grants from two major private foundations and a 1 percent food and beverage tax (Bamberger and Parham, 1984). The city also constructed a world-class natatorium and track and field facilities near the downtown area, as well as one of the few velodromes in the United States (Bamburger and Parham, 1984). These facilities have attracted major sporting events to the city and the outside revenues they bring with them. These events include the 1987 Pan American Games, the 1988 Olympic Trials in several events, and a host of major college and professional sporting contests. The city is now the home office of the NCAA central offices and the NCAA Hall of Champions Museum (Rayner, 2000).

The new amenities developed by public-private partnerships in Indianapolis have not been limited to sports facilities. The old Circle Theatre downtown was rehabilitated for use by the Indianapolis Symphony Orchestra, the former Indiana Theatre was renovated to house the Indiana Repertory Theatre, and the convention center was expanded and linked to the Hoosierdome to allow for very large convention groups (Bamberger and Parham, 1984; Hamlin and Lyons, 1996).

What kinds of central city development was leveraged by these investments in amenity infrastructure? Several major hotels opened in the downtown, including the Union Station Holiday Inn, the Embassy Suites, the Canterbury, the Westin, and Omni Severn (a rehabilitation of the old Atkinson Hotel). City officials estimated that in the mid-1980s, new restaurants were opening up in the downtown area at the rate of one per month. The city's Union Station was renovated and adapted for use as a retail/hotel complex. Several major office buildings were constructed, including the American United Life Building, Market Tower, the twin-towered Capital Center, and the Bank One Center. New housing was constructed in the downtown area and the old Lockerbie Square residential neighborhood, located just east of the downtown, was revitalized, as people moved back into the central city. The enhanced quality of life attracted several major corporations and organizations and induced them to relocate to Indianapolis, including the Dana Corporation, Purolator Courier, Overland Express, and the Hudson Institute (Bamberger and Parham, 1984). All of this private development activity was leveraged by the investment on the part of the city and its charitable organizations in the local amenity infrastructure (Hamlin and Lyons, 1996).

In the mid 1990s the spirit of public-private partnership hibernated. As a result, much of the momentum previously described disappeared. Market Square Arena became obsolete, Union Station, which opened as a festival marketplace in 1986, fell into underutilization and ill repair and closed a decade after it opened, thus affecting the hotel attached to it (Woods, 1999). The new restaurant surge of the 1980s and the construction of new downtown housing flattened out (Welsh, 2000). In 1995 USA Group paid $50 million for a new downtown headquarters for their 600 employees next to the Circle Center Mall. This was after the city paid $10 million to buy the building and fix it up, a direct subsidy and real estate write-down. The city also gave USA Group a ten-year property tax abatement worth over $1 million. The company put $22 million into improvements. For $3.2 million, the company took ownership of Union Station and a garage next to it as part of the deal but turned the station back to the city. Also, the state of Indiana promised to give USA Group its student loan management business as a market stabilization inducement. The deal was a multifaceted public-private partnership that was a coup for the city, but by autumn 1999, USA Group let it be known that they were thinking of leaving downtown. The Union Station area had stagnated and many USA Group employees were unhappy with the downtown location (Albert, 1999).

Early in 2000 a flurry of public-private partnership successes may have regenerated some momentum. Conseco Fieldhouse had just opened, Union Station had reopened as a grand banquet hall, the "greenway," which stretched 7.5 miles, was completed through downtown with a river walk along Old Water Company Canal, Fletcher Place opened as a newly renovated historic building, and the William H. Block Building was being converted to retail and empty-nester apartments. At that time USA Group decided to stay downtown.

The 18,500-seat Conseco Fieldhouse, postmodern in architecture and ultramodern in technology, was a complex public-private partnership deal. The approximately $183 million came from both public and private sources ($104 million private and $79 million public). The Indiana Pacers paid $57 million up front plus user fees. Simons, a parking company, promised $35 million for the right to 1,300 parking spaces. Eli Lilly made a cash contribution of $10 million and allowed the fieldhouse to use its parking spaces nearby. Investors in Circle City Mall, a nearby downtown mall, lent the project $37 million to be paid back by the city over twenty years. Fifty million dollars came from a state-created Pro

Sports Development Authority and a direct state subsidy in the form of a $4.7 million state infrastructure grant (Horgan, 1999).

A look at central Indianapolis over several decades indicates that a large amount of private investment can be leveraged with small government and foundation direct subsidies. Also, momentum must be maintained by focusing on the future and keeping the public and non-profit sector engaged while the private sector implements the vision.

Management

Business Development Assistance

Increasingly, the focus of local economic development efforts has been toward the creation of new enterprises. This approach is both locally sustainable and recognizes the important role that small businesses play in job creation. Many of the entrepreneurs who start new businesses are idea people and/or technical experts who have very little knowledge regarding the day-to-day operations of a business. Indeed, poor management is one of the leading causes of the high rate of failure among new businesses. In response, many local communities have developed programs to provide management and business development assistance to their entrepreneurs. Some of these programs take the form of Small Business Development Centers (SBDCs), business incubation programs, and entrepreneurship training courses. They typically involve participation by local Chambers of Commerce, the Service Corps of Retired Executives (SCORE), local banks, universities, community colleges, and other public, private, and nonprofit organizations (Hamlin and Lyons, 1996).

No matter what their specific structure, all of these business development programs attempt to school entrepreneurs in basic business management skills: finance, budgeting, human resource development, strategic planning, and related subjects. The entrepreneurs' education may take the form of formal training sessions, workshops, seminars, mentoring, and one-on-one consultation. A thriving small business sector is recognized to be in the entire community's best interest.

Feasibility Studies

Public agencies can offer a valuable incentive to private development by preparing feasibility studies for individual firms or entire industries.

Market studies, financial feasibility analyses, fiscal impact studies, or similar investigations help firms make important decisions (NASDA, CUED, and the Urban Institute, 1983). The intention, of course, is to provide the firm or industry with useful information that will enhance its market position while at the same time highlight the assisting locale as a desirable location for investment (Lyons, 1987). Often a public body will have better access to this information and a better understanding of how to use it than private companies will (Hamlin and Lyons, 1996).

Tax Incentives

Tax incentives are also financial inducements to private development. They are aimed at reducing the cost of doing business by decreasing the tax burden on firms that invest in a targeted renewal area. These incentives afford moratoria, exemptions, or abatements on the many varieties of taxation encountered by businesses. Among these are corporate income taxes; use taxes; sales taxes; property taxes on land, plant, equipment, and machinery; excise taxes; and payroll taxes; (NASDA, CUED and the Urban Institute, 1983). Like the incentives intended to abate them, the taxes levied vary by state and municipality (Lyons, 1987; Hamlin and Lyons, 1996).

Exemptions and Abatements

The following represent some of the more commonly used tax incentives (*Site Selection Handbook*, 1985):

- *Special corporate income tax exemptions* excuse the recipient firm(s) from taxation of its profits. This incentive is often used to encourage employment of identified types, or numbers, of workers (NASDA, CUED and the Urban Institute, 1983; Hamlin and Lyons, 1996).

- *Corporate tax abatements*. Enterprise (or business) taxes are levied by the local government in Japan. They are similar to state single business taxes in the United States. These taxes can be reduced by the local government as an incentive to development (Hamlin and Lyons, 1996).

- *Special personal income tax exemptions* are similar to corporate income tax exemptions, except that they pertain to individual income. They are most often directed at small business entrepreneurs to encourage them to utilize more labor or capital by exempting them from taxes on portions of their income (Lyons, 1987; Hamlin and Lyons, 1996).

- *Excise tax exemptions.* Some states levy excise taxes on the consumption of specified goods within those states. They are commonly appropriated on commodities such as gasoline and other fuels (NASDA, CUED, and the Urban Institute, 1983). Excise tax exemptions are intended to reduce operation costs for firms that use large amounts of these commodities (Lyons, 1987; Hamlin and Lyons, 1996).

- *Inventory tax exemptions.* Inventory taxes on goods in transit are, in essence, personal property taxes on items warehoused in the state levying the tax, but intended for delivery to another jurisdiction. States may exempt these goods from inventory taxation by giving them "freeport" status (NASDA, CUED, and the Urban Institute, 1983; Hamlin and Lyons, 1996).

- *Manufacturers' inventory tax exemptions* release firms that store items for use in the production process from paying this form of personal property tax levied by some states. These exemptions are normally reserved for certain specified inventory (Lyons, 1987; Hamlin and Lyons, 1996).

- *Tax exemptions or moratoria on land / capital improvements* and on equipment and machinery are very specific types of tax incentives. They seek to encourage investment in land and capital equipment by exempting firms from property taxes on these production inputs, either indefinitely or for an established time period (Lyons, 1987). The government offering these incentives does so in the hope that the resultant expansion in capital investment will be accompanied by an increase in labor input as well (Lyons, 1987). Governments contemplating use of these incentives for generating new jobs should be aware that they can have a perverse impact on job creation. That is, a reduction in the cost of capital may actually encourage a firm to employ more capital at the expense of labor, depending on the firm's elasticity of demand for labor (Hamlin and Lyons, 1996).

- *Sales and use tax exemptions* on new capital equipment are fairly common tax incentives. Sales taxes are borne by the purchaser and levied on goods sold at retail or wholesale. Use taxes are imposed on the use, consumption, or storage of items not subject to a sales tax (NASDA, CUED, and the Urban Institute, 1983). Exemptions from these taxes seek to stimulate capital expansion on the part of private recipients (Lyons, 1987; Hamlin and Lyons, 1996).

- *Tax stabilization agreements* are another incentive used to attract investment by certain specified industries. These agreements often embody a commitment by the government to limit fluctuations in the amount and type of taxation borne by the selected private sector beneficiaries (Lyons, 1987; Hamlin and Lyons, 1996).

- *Tax exemptions to encourage research and development* represent an increasingly popular form of tax incentive. Greater emphasis on advanced technologies in industry should cause this incentive to continue to grow in importance (Lyons, 1987). The taxes most often included in these exemptions are property taxes, the corporate income tax, and sales and use taxes that impact firms conducting research and development (NASDA, CUED, and the Urban Institute, 1983; Hamlin and Lyons, 1996).

- *Accelerated depreciation* of capital equipment is an indirect tax incentive. This inducement operates on the theory that a firm that can reduce its property tax liability by depreciating its equipment at a faster rate will reinvest those savings in the expansion of its facilities (Lyons, 1987).

- *Tax credits for training the "chronically" unemployed* seek to encourage businesses to invest in training for this segment of the labor force. This incentive is often targeted at large manufacturing or service businesses that employ sizable numbers of semiskilled and unskilled workers (Lyons, 1987; Hamlin and Lyons, 1996).

- *Toka-Kocan system*. Land values in Japan are so high that most development incentive programs tend to be aimed at mitigating this problem or avoiding taxation when land changes hands. *Toka-Kocan*, or equivalent value exchange, is one such incentive. It allows for the legal trade of real estate with no sales or capital gains taxes. The land is then owned by the developer and the original landowner in some proportion (e.g., 65 percent owned by developer, 35 percent owned by original landowner). The relationship between the two parties is a partnership of sorts, but the original landowner bears no liability (Hamlin and Lyons, 1996).

Enterprise Zones

Enterprise zones represent another type of development inducement employing tax incentives. The concept of the enterprise zone was originally developed in Great Britain by Peter Hall and was aimed at freeing private businesses, located within certain geographic areas, from government regulation (Sidor, 1982, pp. 1–2). This approach has been adjusted in the United States to consist of the designation of low-income, high unemployment urban areas for redevelopment. Within these "zones," economic revitalization is encouraged via a package of tax incentives that is intended to stimulate development and, hence, the creation of new jobs (Sidor, 1982). Several states in the United States have adopted enterprise zone legislation. There is considerable variation in zone size, eligibility requirements, and zone incentives across the states, making it difficult to generalize about the nature of these entities (Sidor, 1982; Hamlin and Lyons, 1996).

In concept, enterprise zones also employ the relaxation of some development regulations as a further incentive to development within the zone. In practice, this feature is controversial and legally complex, although the incentives built into land use laws can be emphasized within the zone. A somewhat modified version of the enterprise zone concept was implemented by the Clinton administration in the United States and carries the name "empowerment zone."

Tax Increment Financing (TIF)

TIF combines the elements of several of the public-private partnership activities discussed in this book. This development financing technique is commonly used in deteriorated urban areas to spur redevelopment. The unique aspect of TIF is that, from the public sector standpoint, the cost of inducing development is borne by all the taxing jurisdictions affecting the redevelopment area in proportion to the increase in property tax revenues they receive as a result of redevelopment (Huddleston, 1981; Hamlin and Lyons, 1996).

For a city to engage in TIF, the state in which it is located must have enacted specific enabling legislation for this purpose. The particulars of this enabling legislation vary from state to state, but follow a basic form. The city begins by establishing a TIF district. This may range in size from a single city block up to an entire central business district. The city is normally required to prepare an inventory of the land uses, zoning, and building stock for the district and a redevelopment plan for approval before the TIF process can proceed. Assessments for the district are frozen at their present value (American Planning Association, 1976). This affects all taxing jurisdictions that include the designated TIF district. The combined assessed valuation of all the property in the TIF district is the "base value" of the district (Hamlin and Lyons, 1996).

The city, through its tax increment finance authority (TIFA), can acquire land and make capital improvements in the district (e.g., streets, lighting, landscaping, etc.) to make it more desirable to developers. It can also offer additional incentives to private development in the area of the kinds discussed in this chapter. When development occurs, the value of the real property in the district increases. This increased value is taxed, but for the period of time during which the TIF district is in effect, the tax revenues resulting from the increment in value go to the TIFA not the other taxing jurisdictions. These additional taxes not distributed to other taxing jurisdictions are the *tax increment*. The TIF authority uses the tax increment to pay off the expenses incurred by the city in land acquisition and the installation of capital improvements (Huddleston, 1981). (For an example of how TIF works, see Lyons and Hamlin, 1991, p. 108, or Huddleston, 1981, pp. 374–376.)

The TIF concept is increasingly used for all kinds of development and redevelopment projects. In Michigan, for example, TIF powers are given to downtown development authorities and brownfield redevelopment authorities to provide resources for site cleanup (Hula, 1999).

Markets

Market Stabilization

One way for the public sector to induce the private sector to act in desired ways is for the government to be a guaranteed buyer of the private sector's product. A real estate example of this is the situation in which government, in exchange for desired developer behavior, promises to rent some portion of a development project for a guaranteed period of time at an agreed on price. If the local municipality needs to expand its city hall floor area, for example, one approach might be to rent space from the private sector rather than to build a new government building. This can be a real plum to offer a developer of a project who is willing to cooperate by developing according to the plan of the city. Even if the city only rents a small portion of an office building project, the resulting income stability can significantly reduce the risk of the project for the developer (Hamlin and Lyons, 1996). If an office tower were structured as an office condominium, the city could float public purpose tax-exempt general obligation bonds to buy part of the office condo, thus guaranteeing the developer an immediate return on at least part of the investment (Hamlin and Lyons, 1996).

Programs to Increase Export

Governments sometimes provide technical assistance to private firms wishing to market their products internationally (Lyons, 1987). This assistance includes information on trade opportunities abroad, help in creating linkages with foreign buyers, assistance in organizing trade shows, guidance in accessing federal exporting resources, and direct marketing assistance (Long, 1984). This incentive can be used by government to encourage firms to locate in declining urban areas and expand their production, and, hence, their operations. It can also be used as part of a package of inducements to lure private firms into investing in new operations in local communities (Hamlin and Lyons, 1996).

Federal Contract Procurement

The federal government in the United States lets numerous contracts to private firms. While defense spending is the largest part of the federal budget, the federal government purchases all kinds of products, from soap to shoes. These contracts can be quite lucrative. Large firms, particularly those that have been awarded contracts previously, have a decided advantage in the competition for new contracts due to their familiarity with the process and better information on contract availability. Governmental assistance in obtaining procurement information, bidding on contracts, and managing contracts can help to spread the benefit of federal procurement to a large base of firms, and induce firms to develop in declining areas (Hamlin and Lyons, 1996).

Research

These programs offer research assistance in the form of expert consultation, both public and private, including appropriate faculty from public universities and community colleges. This may be taken a step further by making public university R&D facilities available for use by private firms (Lyons, 1987). With the proliferation of urban branches of major state universities over the past twenty-five years, this incentive becomes particularly useful for promoting central city redevelopment. Many governments collect, retain, disseminate, and update data that are helpful to industrial R&D efforts (Lyons, 1987; Hamlin and Lyons, 1996).

Project Coordination Function

As the final activity discussed in this section, project coordination really amounts to focusing and integrating all the activities already mentioned in a specifically defined project area. A hypothetical scenario is as follows. First, land is acquired or the cooperative participation of private property owners is assured. Second, property lines are redrawn to produce more useful parcels and better transportation access. This may involve land readjustment or public sector condemnation and replatting. Third, public sector improvements are planned and implemented. This may mean that only physical infrastructure improvements are made to modernize the project area and prepare it for development. It may mean that a public or quasi-public anchor project is completed, such as a convention center in a hotel district, an airport in an air industrial park, or a riverfront plaza in a downtown. Fourth, the feasibility of various private development alternatives is investigated. The feasibility of a project may require assurances of the success of the anchor and/or additional financial or other incentives (Hamlin and Lyons, 1996). Fifth, publicly owned land is sold to private developers at below market prices if the buyers are willing to develop the project within the project planning guidelines. Sixth, private owners are induced to build in accordance with the project plan because of regulator incentives such as TDRs or benefits they received from property line readjustments, infrastructure improvements, improvements in surrounding developments, or other incentives. Seventh, labor force recruitment and training services are offered to prospective new and expanding businesses. Eighth, where the public sector is the buyer of products or the renter of space, market stabilization agreements with private firms may be appropriate. Ninth, financial incentives are focused on the project area, including debt and equity capital or other forms of risk sharing. Tenth, tax breaks ranging from enterprise zones to industrial development property tax abatements to income tax credits are concentrated in the project area. Eleventh, export promotion, marketing assistance, and the entire package of potential governmental incentive and business incubation programs may be focused in the project area.

The key concept here is to focus incentives and public-private risk sharing in the project area to the degree necessary to create a synergistic critical mass or "tipping point strategy" (Gladwell, 1996) such that achievement of public goals and private return on investment is relatively assured and private investment flows in. This is no easy task. One of the failures of urban policy has been to underestimate what is required to reverse negative externalities and create positive synergy in declining urban settings (Hamlin and Lyons, 1996).

NOTE

The material in this chapter is an expansion of that presented in Chapter 4 of Roger E. Hamlin and Thomas S. Lyons, *Economy Without Walls: Managing Local Development in a Restructuring World* (New York: Praeger, 1996).

4

The Economic Development Program

Having established a set of measurable objectives, gathered basic information to be used in plan formation, and developed an understanding of the concept of public-private partnership and its role in economic development, the next step is to translate the general to the specific, to determine what actions should be taken during the next planning cycle. This chapter does so in two parts. The first part describes the layout or format of an action plan, while the second discusses some specific actions that have worked in other communities.

ACTION PLAN FORMAT

The following are the major components of an action plan, discussed in the order in which they should be addressed in the plan. Each subsection contains sample wording from a simplified action plan statement.

The Action Statement

The principal component of the action plan format is the action statement. An action statement is a one- or two-sentence statement that describes an action to be taken by some agent in the community. Embodied in the action statement is a specific reference to the actor or

agent. The actor should be somebody under the power of the governmental body, or some private sector entity that has expressed a clear
willingness, under certain conditions, to carry out the proposed action.
It does little good in an action plan to state that actions will be carried
out by actors who have expressed no willingness to cooperate and over
whom local authorities exert no leverage. If a particular segment of the
private sector should behave in a certain way, then the action statement should read, "The city will take action xyz which will induce sector
abc to behave in manner 123." To simply express the hope that the
participants will behave in the desired manner is not an action plan. A
simple example of an action statement might be as follows: "The public
works department of the city of Dansville will build a visitor center on
the property owned by the city at the I-82 interchange on Howe Road."

Description

After stating the action and actor at the outset, provide a more complete description of the action. This description should be brief and
should not discuss the effects of the action. At this stage, the action
may be general enough to allow flexibility in the way it is implemented.
Using the visitor center action statement as an example, the description might be as follows:

> The center will be large enough for individuals to drive up and
> walk inside to see displays about the city, its shops, industry, tour-
> ist sites, and general livability. The most important feature of the
> center is that it be very attractive. The second most important
> characteristic is that it convey information. Information should
> primarily include items related to the visitor (lodging, restau-
> rants, attractions, points of interest, and reasons for visiting). Sec-
> ond, it should list the shops that are available. Information should
> also include data about the industrial products and business po-
> tential of the community and the community's interest in further
> business development.
>
> Information should be communicated through a variety of me-
> dia, including handout literature, pictures, slideshows, videos,
> and movies. To the extent possible, the centers should be auto-
> mated and have the capacity to be unstaffed. A telephone could
> offer free local calls to the visitor center in Dansville and to local

motels and restaurants. This approach could greatly reduce the cost of operations.

Location

If the action has a specific location or locations, this factor might be indicated in the description, or in a separate section. Maps should be used where appropriate. The location statement for the visitor center could read as follows: "Lot 15 of the Howe Subdivision #2 owned by the city of Dansville. See map and site plan."

Process

For a complex action, a separate section, longer than the brief description, describes the step-by-step process for carrying out the action and indicates a timetable for completion of steps. This statement can still be somewhat general and flexible. One of the steps of the described process may be to formulate detailed plans, budgets, and timetables. Continuing the visitor center example, an abbreviated process statement is as follows:

1. Since the property is already owned by the city, the first step is to draw a preliminary site plan illustrating the location of the building, parking, landscaping, and so on (three weeks).

2. Once the preliminary site plan has been approved, detailed construction drawings of the building can be completed (nine weeks).

*   *   *

45. Visitor center will be dedicated and begin operation (one week for preparation).

Results

The next section should describe the intended results of the action to be taken. This should primarily justify the action on terms of the measurable objectives of the action plan using the data available. Some background to the problem or need for the program is appropriate here. For the visitor center, the "results" section is as follows:

Recently, a large amount of development has been constructed at the I-82 Howe Rd. interchange. These projects create several opportunities and potential problems for economic expansion in Dansville. Because this development attracts people from other major metropolitan areas, and because it induces I-82 traffic to exit at Howe, this new development may generate increased visitor traffic for downtown Dansville and augment its visibility. Although the new construction on Howe feeds off Dansville visitor traffic, it also draws a distinct clientele from which Dansville might benefit.

Congestion around this interchange could reduce accessibility to Dansville, frustrating the achievement of one of the important objectives of the economic development plan. It may discourage Dansville traffic, and stores around the interchanges may compete with shops in central Dansville.

To attempt to maximize the benefits of the new development while minimizing problems, the Dansville visitor center should be established near the interchange.

A visitor center attracts the attention of visitors, reminds people that Dansville is close, and conveys the appropriate image of Dansville. One of the community's needs, according to the statement of measurable objectives, is for Dansville to expand its image to include a greater emphasis on industrial development. A second need is to expand markets for the products of the community. The center can be used to communicate the Dansville community's interest in and capacity for a much broader array of economic activities. Through appropriate displays and information, the visitor could learn about the goods and services that are produced in Dansville, the market for those products, related economic activities that would be encouraged to locate there, the incentive programs and services available to prospective businesses, and the importance of Dansville to the economy of the region.

Finance

The next point to cover for each action is the finances involved. This includes: (1) the cost of carrying out the action; (2) who has to pay the cost; (3) what sources of financing are available; and (4) what revenues might be generated by the action. As an example:

Construction costs are estimated to be $100 per square foot. Installation and interior decoration would cost approximately $40,000. Annual maintenance is estimated at $20 per square foot. While land is free, the opportunity cost is significant since the lot has a prime location. Construction and operation are to be paid by the city, with a small grant from the Chamber of Commerce covering 10 percent of the cost and a grant from the Enfield Foundation for $10,000. Some revenues may be generated by selling advertising space to businesses, but this is expected to be minimal.

Secondary Impacts

This section should be a brief discussion of the ramifications of carrying out the action. It may contain a variety of both positive and negative unintended effects. Including this section in the action plan indicates that the multitude of impacts of any action have been considered and are understood to the extent possible.

ECONOMIC DEVELOPMENT STRATEGIES

This section contains a description of some economic development programs or actions that communities have found successful. The programs presented are not just mechanisms for attracting industries or providing jobs, but represent imaginative approaches to satisfying the needs of existing as well as prospective firms. The bias is toward development from within, and the economic goals to be achieved are broad. Each program section describes the program, its purpose, how it works, its advantages for business and to the community, which communities currently use the program, and what it takes to be successful.

Business Incubation Program

What Is It?

A business incubation program is a tool for encouraging the formation, survival, and growth of new enterprises. Such a program typically takes one of three forms: (1) a residential incubator, which is a building or set of buildings that has been subdivided for rental to a number of small fledgling businesses and offers flexible work spaces and low-cost support services to these tenants; (2) a virtual incubator, or incubator-without-walls, which is a vehicle for networking local or regional enterprise development service providers to assist entrepreneurs in that geographic area, regardless of their specific location; or (3) a hybrid of these two, which is commonly referred to as an incubator with an affiliates program. This latter arrangement includes an incubator facility, which also makes its support services available for a fee to small businesses located outside the facility.

What Is Its Purpose?

The purpose of a business incubation program is to promote the success of small businesses by helping them minimize overhead, find needed financing, improve management skills, pool resources and risk, and, ultimately, move out into the world to function on their own. Put another way, the incubation program's mission is to help entrepreneurs overcome the obstacles they face to acquiring the resources they require for business success (Lichtenstein and Lyons, 1996). This support is commonly offered during the first two to five years of the new firm's existence, the most crucial period in its ultimate survival.

Who Operates an Incubation Program?

Incubation programs can be owned and operated by public, non-profit, or for-profit organizations. Public operators may include city or county governments, state governments, community colleges, or state-supported research universities, among others. In recent years the largest percentage of incubation programs have been operated by nonprofit entities, such as community development corporations, economic development corporations, industrial development authorities, or other public-private partnerships. The last few years have witnessed a sharp rise in the number of privately owned and operated programs. These sponsors include private corporations, chambers of commerce, real estate development companies, or privately held community development banks, to name a few.

How Does It Work?

The first step in the development of an incubation program is to establish the organization itself. No matter how the organization is structured, the key to success in this and future steps is to find a strong program manager and identify a dedicated and competent board of directors. Most important, the manager must be experienced and knowledgeable in business development. Managers must also work well with people. These skills are essential no matter what form the incubation program assumes. Managers of residential incubators are expected to have property management skills as well. In selecting a board of directors, care must be taken to identify those individuals who bring needed skills and connections to the program. A viable board might include, among others, someone with business development expertise, another from local government, a representative of the local corporate community, and a successful entrepreneur.

The second step is to raise initial financing for the program. Incubation programs are relatively low-cost economic development tools. Of course, the start-up costs for a residential incubator are substantially higher than they are for an incubator-without-walls. Financing can come from a variety of sources. As an example, the Enterprise Development Group, a residential incubator in Louisville, Kentucky, drew upon funds from city, state, and local agencies as well as grants from private foundations for its initial financing.

The third step is to purchase and remodel or rehabilitate a building, or to build a new building for use as an incubator. This, of course, applies only to programs with residential components. The decision as to whether to retrofit an existing building or build a new one should take into consideration such factors as cost, the availability of suitable existing structures, and the types of businesses to be incubated and their space and equipment needs. Incubators tend to serve particular types of clients: some are manufacturing or light assembly oriented, others focus on service businesses, still others have a retail focus, while some mix business types (e.g., service and light assembly). The type of building used and its configuration should be based on the needs of the client entrepreneurs to be served, and not the other way around.

Step four is to lease space in the building to appropriate small businesses that have been screened for their readiness (i.e., having a viable business plan), show compatibility with the mission of the incubator and with other tenants, demonstrate potential for creating jobs, and other considerations. The number of tenants will vary depending on the size of the local economy, nature of the tenant businesses, and the level of the incubator's recruitment effort. Traditionally, rents have been the chief source of revenue for incubators and they still make an important contribution; however, with the creation of new sources (e.g., fees from affiliate clients, taking equity positions in tenant firms, etc.), rents have become only one of a variety of such sources. Formerly, incubators charged their tenants below market rents. Now, most incubators have successfully argued that they provide so much additional value to their clients through their other services that the vast majority charge market rental rates. Incubator operators usually write complex leases that look something like a mall lease. The lease contains rent (often graduated over time) to cover space, some additions to rent to cover standard shared services, and a volume-based fee to cover variable cost services such as copying and phone answering.

The current trend in incubation is to attempt to achieve financial self-sufficiency through various means. While this may be appealing to sponsors, it might ultimately be detrimental to incubator tenants and clients, as more of the burden of financing the program is being placed on these businesses. This could be especially onerous for clients of incubation programs that serve low-income and minority entrepreneurs. In some cases, a certain level of subsidization of incubator activities may be necessary in perpetuity. Rather than viewing this as a form of small business "welfare," program sponsors should think of it as an investment in their community's economic health.

Step five is to set up joint services to be shared among the various client businesses so as to reduce their start-up overhead. These shared services might include:

reception service

clerical assistance

unskilled labor such as delivery personnel

use of basic equipment ranging from forklift trucks to facsimile machines to microcomputers

printing and copying services

communication services such as internet access and video conferencing capability

day care for employees' children

security services

market and industry research

laboratory or kitchen facilities

truck loading dock

office furniture rental

common conference and lunch rooms

bookkeeping and checkbook balancing

Fees for these services can be built into rental rates by residential in-cubation programs, as mentioned previously. Operators of virtual and affiliates programs will need to develop a separate fee structure.

The sixth step is to provide financial assistance to client businesses. This may take a variety of forms. Some incubation programs help by preparing their clients to go to traditional lenders (i.e., commercial banks). They employ such practices as helping to refine the business plan or taking the client through simulations of a meeting with a banker in order to help her prepare her case.

Another form of financial assistance is the provision of seed capital. Seed capital can be either debt or equity capital and varies depending on the nature of the small business, its needs, and the risk involved. Seed capital can be in any amount from $500 (in the case of some mi-croenterprises) to $300,000. It is crucial to a start-up business's success because of the variety of costs faced by the business prior to the time that sales revenues meet expenses (see "Seed Capital" in Chapter 2).

The incubation program can provide seed capital in several ways. It can consider direct loans to small businesses as part of incubator op-erations. Charging below-market rent or offering rent rebates are forms of in-kind seed capital. If a municipal agency or authority manages the incubator, it may locate the office of the local revolving loan fund there. Some incubation programs operate their own revolving loan funds.

Seed capital is not the only form of capital assistance provided by some incubation programs. Many programs are now taking equity po-sitions in their client businesses. This is particularly true of those pro-grams with high technology and technology transfer focuses. The Arizona Technology Incubator (ATI) in Scottsdale offers an excellent example of this approach (Hamlin and Lyons, 1996). Some technology-oriented incubators, like the MGE Innovation Center in Madison, Wis-consin, host the offices of a venture capital firm in their facilities. This allows the venture capitalists and the entrepreneurs to get to know one another, hopefully resulting in mutual benefit to both.

Step seven in the organization of an incubation program is to provide business management assistance. Management assistance can take the form of seminars on such subjects as accounting, taxes, seed capital, marketing, procurement, use of computer technology in business, work-ers' compensation, unemployment compensation, and liability insur-ance. If the community has a one-stop shopping program of business information and services, it helps to locate this program in the residen-tial incubator. A number of incubators around the United States are home to the local Small Business Development Center (SBDC). Management assistance may also take the form of individualized assistance through coaching by the incubation program manager and/or mentoring by local business people. For example, an incubation program in a rural community in Minnesota asks the members of its board of directors to serve as mentors to its client entrepreneurs (Lichtenstein and Lyons, 1996). Many incubation program managers cite managerial assistance as the most important service they provide. Poor management is the leading killer of small businesses, particularly in their first three to five years after start up. Most incubation program clients are entrepreneurs with a business concept and the technical skills to make it work, but who lack general management expertise.

An asset that every established incubation program has but often underutilizes is its graduates, those firms that were once clients in the incubation program and have successfully moved on. These firms can play a variety of roles in incubating current tenants and affiliates. They can share their experience with neophyte enterprises through a graduate mentor program. They may act as purchasers of goods and services produced by current clients. They might also serve as role models for what can be accomplished, providing hope and inspiration to beleaguered newcomers.

What Are the Advantages to the Community?

If the community directly or indirectly operates the incubation program, it can require a promise from graduating businesses that they will stay in town for a specified period of time. The community therefore experiences an increase in employment. Employment generated by incubation programs can broaden the economic base of the community and make it less susceptible to economic cycles. Some businesses in the community benefit from sales to the successful new businesses. Others enjoy the benefits of having new local suppliers, cutting costs associated with purchasing from vendors outside the community in some cases, or increasing productive competition among local firms.

Residential incubators that use existing buildings employ unused or underutilized space in the community and can effectively create jobs for and give vitality to deteriorating parts of town. They are especially effective economic development tools in small communities because of their sustainability in smaller economies.

Where Is It Used?

In 1984, the U.S. Small Business Administration estimated that over 200 incubation programs operated in the United States. The most recent estimate by the National Business Incubation Association (NBIA) puts that figure at over 600. Thus, in the past fifteen years, according to this source, incubation programs have tripled in number (NBIA, 1995). Yet, incubation programs are assuming such diverse forms that they are difficult to count, implying that many more have yet to be identified.

As might be expected, the largest states are among those that had the most incubation programs that were members of the NBIA in 1995. Pennsylvania had 56 such programs; New York had 35; California had 27; and Texas had 26. Pennsylvania has long been considered a leading state in small business incubation. However, mid-sized and smaller states have also been very active in the incubation arena. Wisconsin had twenty-nine NBIA member programs in 1995, while Oklahoma had fifteen (NBIA, 1995).

Business incubation programs can be found in urban, suburban, and rural locations. While most programs are found in urban areas, the rural sector of the incubation industry has grown rapidly in recent years.

What Does It Take to Make It Successful?

Based on the experience to date, a priority list of the most important components of a successful incubation program, in terms of its ability to serve its clients, would generally seem to be a reverse ordering of the steps listed above. That is, the provision of high-quality management assistance seems to be the most important in promoting successful small businesses. Small businesses fail at a high rate and a study by the Comprehensive Accounting Corporation indicates that poor management and related problems explain most small business failures. New small businesses underestimate costs, competition, and the need for marketing, and are overly optimistic about economic situations. They tend to know little about finance, personnel management, and legal obstacles. Helping new entrepreneurs develop skills in these areas goes a long way toward increasing business success.

The second most important service provided by the incubation program is that of financing assistance. The third most important is shared services. In many respects, the least important component of the incubation program is the building itself. As discussed above, it is possible to run a decentralized program that provides management and financial assistance to businesses occupying space anywhere in the community.

From the perspective of the internal operations of a successful incubation program, strong management in the form of a capable program manager and a qualified board of directors is crucial. Furthermore, in incubation, as in good architecture, form should follow function. Everything from the configuration of the building to the design of the assistance package offered should be determined by the needs of the client entrepreneurs: helping them to overcome the obstacles they face acquiring essential resources for success.

Microenterprise Programs for Disadvantaged Communities

What Is It?

A microenterprise program is a local enterprise development tool designed to assist low-income entrepreneurs and self-employed individuals. Although microenterprise programs vary considerably in terms of their missions, goals, and designs (Friedman and Sahay, 1996), most consist of two component parts: a micro loan program and a business development program. The micro loan program makes small loans of $25,000 or less to program clients. The business development program offers training in various business management skills.

Microenterprise programs in the United States have their roots in the micro loan program of the Grameen Bank of Bangladesh, founded in 1976 and aimed at assisting poor, self-employed women (Rahman, 1999). Shortly after implementing micro lending in the United States, it became apparent to practitioners that merely providing small loans to entrepreneurs and the self-employed was not enough to enhance their success. Too many start-up efforts by micro lending program clients failed due to nonexistent or poorly developed business management skills on the part of the client. This led to the creation of microenterprise programs that provide both loans and business development assistance under one roof. In 1996, it was estimated that there were over 500 microenterprise programs operating throughout the United States (Friedman and Sahay, 1996), and that number has continued to increase.

What Is Its Purpose?

The purpose of a microenterprise program is to provide access to capital, business development skill-building assistance, and (most recently) markets to low-income individuals who seek to start a business

(Friedman and Sahay, 1996). Most of these individuals are self-employed, some by choice, but many by necessity created by corporate layoffs or welfare-to-work requirements. These individuals typically do not have access to the more traditional sources of start-up capital available to mainstream entrepreneurs (e.g., credit cards, second mortgage on a home, loans from family members, etc.). They are also less likely to obtain loans from traditional lending institutions due to poor credit, inability to pay interest rates, lack of collateral, or transaction barriers such as race, gender, limited ability to speak and write in English, and so forth (Lichtenstein and Lyons, 1996). They may also face similar transaction barriers to obtaining access to entrepreneurial skills-building assistance and to markets. Microenterprise programs are designed to address these obstacles to business creation success.

Also, recent emphasis on an asset-orientation to community development and social service delivery adds to the importance of micoenterprise development. Asset-oriented community development focuses on the strengths of individuals and communities (Kretzman and McKnight, 1993). The traditional deficit model implies that outside professionals identify all of the problems faced by an individual or neighborhood and employ outsider-provided deficit mitigating services to help those perceived to be in need. An asset approach starts by identifying what people are proud of about themselves and their community and works first to build and enable those strengths by overcoming barriers to achieving personal goals such as those related to knowledge and finance (Hamlin, 1999). Some research suggests that an asset approach is a far better way to promote community and individual independence. Reasons include: (1) the approach better involves people in their own development, (2) the method promotes self-esteem, (3) it provides people and communities with hope, future goals, and resulting enthusiasm, and (4) the development of personal assets often naturally reduces deficits (Keith and Perkins, 1996). Microenterprise development may, in some cases, be the perfect nexus between community social development and local economic development in disadvantaged communities.

The businesses started by self-employed individuals constitute as much as three-quarters of all new business start-ups in the United States each year (Scheer and Reynolds, 1999). This would tend to indicate that the demand, and need, for assistance to these microentrepreneurs is quite high, particularly in economically disadvantaged communities. Thus, a microenterprise program can play an important role in these communities as a tool for both economic and community development. It can help to create employment and build wealth in terms of assets as well as income (Oliver and Shapiro, 1997).

Who Operates a Microenterprise Program?

Microenterprise programs may be operated by any of a number of public and/or nonprofit entities. Most often they are programs of community development corporations (CDCs) or other community-based organizations (CBOs), including religious establishments. Others are operated by local governments.

Microenterprise programs are sponsored by a variety of entities as well. Local banks may provide money for their revolving loan funds. Local governments may also provide financial assistance. State governments may supply funds for furnishing business and technical assistance. Some federal programs exist that support microenterprise development as well. In particular, the U.S. Small Business Administration maintains a program (the Micro-Loan Demonstration Program) that provides selected microenterprise programs with funds for making loans up to $25,000 to their clients. The Aspen Institute of Washington, D.C., operates a program known as FIELD (Fund for Innovation, Effectiveness, Learning and Dissemination), which makes grants targeted to microenterprise programs to assist them in capacity-building activities.

How Does It Work?

Because microenterprise programs vary so much in their specific missions and structures, it is difficult to describe a prototypical program. However, it may be useful to specify a successful program as an example. The Business Plus Microenterprise Program operates in the economically disadvantaged neighborhoods of the west side of Louisville, Kentucky. It was the first comprehensive microenterprise program established in that state. Its clients are principally low-income and African American, and predominately women (Durr, Lyons, and Cornwell, 1998).

Unlike many microenterprise programs, Business Plus did not begin as a micro loan program. Instead, it started in 1992 as a training program for business plan development, which was the forerunner of the present day Business Plus Training Institute. In 1994, Business Plus began developing its micro lending capacity with a $25,000 grant from the Louisville-Jefferson County Office for Economic Development, the local public economic development agency at that time. This permitted Business Plus to create its Micro-Loan Program. Thus, Business Plus has developed separate business and technical training and micro lending divisions within its organization that it has linked in appropriate ways (Durr, Lyons, and Cornwell, 1998).

The Training Institute is designed to deliver business skill development and technical training in a group-oriented, supportive environment. Using a framework created by Lichtenstein and Lyons (1996), Business Plus assesses its clients' entrepreneurial skills on entering the program, which, in turn, permits the program to track each client into a strategic and appropriate training regimen. Training is provided in a comprehensive array of business subjects: marketing, management, accounting/bookkeeping, strategic planning, and so on. While some of the instruction is conducted by Business Plus staff, most of it is offered by volunteer professionals from the community. Strong interaction among clients, staff, and volunteers is encouraged in order to provide the training in an emotionally supportive environment (Durr, Lyons, and Cornwell, 1998). This approach builds social capital within the microenterprise program and a bridge from dependence to independence. A large number of the Training Institute's clients are not Business Plus lendees—they are merely availing themselves of the training opportunity. Those who are receiving micro loans, however, must honor their commitment to a specified minimum of forty hours of training or they will be considered in default on their loans.

The micro lending side of Business Plus made its first loans in 1994. Originally, the peer lending model created by the Grameen Bank was employed exclusively. Under this model, clients are placed in small (peer) groups of four to seven. A revolving loan fund of $10,000 is established for each group. The peer group is made responsible for activities that included client screening, loan application review, loan repayment collection, and technical assistance (Durr, Lyons, and Cornwell, 1998). The ability of each client to obtain additional and/or larger loans is based on the overall credit performance of the peer group, bringing peer pressure to bear on everyone for complete and timely loan repayment. No Business Plus client is eligible to obtain a loan until they have completed a business plan and have formally committed to taking forty hours of training, as previously described. Peer groups make one or two loans at a time. When it is demonstrated that these loans are being repaid in a timely manner, additional loans to peer group members are made (Durr, Lyons, and Cornwell, 1998). As one might imagine, given the small loan fund, peer group loans are quite small.

When Business Plus received a $250,000 grant from the U.S. Small Business Administration's Micro-Loan Demonstration Program, the microenterprise program was able to provide direct lending as a second option for clients. Under direct lending, the program makes loans directly to the microentrepreneur without the peer group apparatus. These loans can range from $5,000 to $25,000. The requirements for loan eligibility are similar to those for the peer lending program. The Business Plus Loan Review Committee, made up of community volunteers, reviews each loan application and evaluates it based on established criteria. Rejected applications are accompanied by very specific descriptions of their shortcomings, and applicants are given the opportunity to correct these deficiencies and resubmit (Durr, Lyons, and Cornwell, 1998).

Although direct lending can be very effective in and of itself, Business Plus has recognized the benefits of peer group interaction and has initiated a program that provides these latter advantages to its direct lendees. The Industry Growth Groups (IGG) program is aimed at bringing together microentrepreneurs in the same industry to engage in networking activities that permit idea-sharing, the pooling of resources, and the joint pursuit of market opportunities, among others. Business Plus has developed IGGs in business services, commercial and construction contracting, fine art/folk art, personal and salon services, and specialized retail. Groups have also been created around functional activities, such as financial management, human resources, investment, marketing, and technology. In order to encourage participation in IGGs, Business Plus allows its lendees to count their participation toward the established training requirements.

What Are the Advantages to the Community?

In the period from 1992 to 1997, Business Plus served over 334 client businesses by providing micro loans and/or business training. It made a total of fifty-four loans, with a repayment rate of 97.5 percent, which is about 5 percent above the national average. Of the fifty-four businesses that received loans, fifty-two were minority-owned and thirty-eight were women-owned. In the process, 192 jobs were created and retained by the businesses that received the loans (Durr, Lyons, and Cornwell, 1998). This suggests that, when well managed, microenterprise programs can be successful tools for enhancing the economies of disadvantaged communities.

Where Is It Used?

Microenterprise programs can be found throughout the United States and the world.

Capital Access Program

What Is It?

The Capital Access Program is a state or local government program that implements a loan insurance pool concept (Hamlin and Lyons, 1996). In situations in which a proposed small business loan carries too much risk for conventional bank financing, various stakeholders deposit money into a fund that is used to back the loan. Over time, with many such deposits, the fund grows. This pool of money is then used to provide backing for a portfolio including all participating loans. This loan loss insurance allows and induces lenders to take on slightly riskier small business loans than they otherwise would. The sponsoring government becomes involved in the creation of the program and in sharing some of the risk (Michigan Jobs Commission, 1996).

What Is Its Purpose?

The purpose of the Capital Access Program is to develop the local economy by promoting small business success. It accomplishes this by inducing lenders to provide more financing to medium-risk businesses, particularly those that can be considered "almost bankable" (Osborne and Plasterik, 1997).

In order to fully employ the labor force and diversify the local economic base, a community must promote a wide variety of businesses in terms of size, age, industry, level of technology, and level of risk. An important part of that strategy is having various forms of business finance available to serve diverse needs (Peek and Rosengren, 1998). Traditional sources of financial capital are not easily available to many kinds of firms. Particularly troublesome is support for the middle range of the risk/reward spectrum (Kimbal, 1997). By establishing loan insurance pools to cover riskier loans, the Capital Access Program works to make capital available to almost bankable middle-risk companies. These are businesses that are sound or have good potential for success, but are not able to receive conventional bank financing. Typically, they have minor collateral problems, and face bankers who are collateral lenders (Mann, 1997).

An example of such a situation is a very small, successful business that must buy expensive, specialized machinery to modernize and compete. This circumstance creates the need for a loan, but their bank is reluctant to provide it. The loan officer does not fully value the machinery as collateral since it would be difficult to resell in the event of dissolution. Another example is a successful winery with much of its finances tied up in "work in progress." The wine in process will someday be valuable but has little current worth in the event of foreclosure. A third example is a temporary employment agency that needs a cash flow line of credit. The business must cover the cash flow gap between the time it pays the temporary employees' salaries and the time it collects from the client firm that used the temp workers. This is a definite cash flow need but the firm has no collateral to offer. Moreover, a service firm (such as a life insurance agency) whose only collateral is illiquid financial paper may also have difficulty qualifying for a conventional bank loan. Many of these financing problems are most severe during periods of success and rapid growth. The loan insurance acts as additional collateral support, allowing for some of these loans to be made and thus enabling local businesses to grow and succeed (Hamlin, 1998).

Who Operates a Capital Access Program?

Most Capital Access Programs were created by states, although two cities have their own programs (U.S. Treasury, 1998). In general, the operating government only sets up the system and turns it over, with as little bureaucratic intervention as possible, to banks. Invariably, the first contact a business has with the program is through its bank, not through the government or an economic development agency (Hamlin, 1998). All terms of the loan are negotiated between the bank and the business including other fees, interest rates, term, additional collateral, and personal guarantees. Government typically does not second-guess the bank's underwriting standards for loan eligibility or its negotiated decisions about loan structure under CAP. Thus, governments create the structure, banks operate the program for their customers, and the competitive marketplace manages the details.

How Does It Work?

To begin, a state (or other legal jurisdiction) must establish a program. Then it recruits banks and/or other financial institutions to participate. For each participating lender the government sets up a CAP insurance fund, or loan loss reserve pool. While legally owned by the government, the fund is typically deposited into the bank that it serves.

The state may prime the pump by making an initial deposit into the fund (U.S. Treasury, 1998). A business that needs a loan will shop for one in its normal way. Typically, it will start with the bank where it most often does business (Berger and Udell, 1995). When a business requests a loan, the bank may determine that the loan application is not conventionally bankable because of collateral gaps. Yet the lender comprehends that the business is fairly sound and a valuable customer. The bank may then offer CAP program participation to the loan applicant (Hamlin, 1998). In this case the bank would notify the business of the extra CAP fees of approximately 3 to 7 percent of the loan proceeds. All other terms of the loan are negotiated by the bank and the business in the normal way, without state intervention.

At this point market forces prevail. If the loan applicant receives a better offer at another bank, he or she may purse the alternative deal. However, if the first bank offers the best loan, even with the extra CAP fees, the business may choose to participate in the CAP program. The CAP fees are then paid by the business and deposited into the bank's CAP fund. The state matches the fee amount with its own deposit into the fund. Some states make bigger contributions in the early years of a bank's participation to help build up the pool (Michigan Jobs Commission, 1996). Also, some governments "target" the program by making larger contributions to the fund if the business is woman or minority owned or in a targeted geographic area such as an enterprise/ empowerment zone (U.S. Treasury, 1998). In some states, the bank must also match the business contribution with a payment into the pool (Hamlin, 1998). The loan is then set up and used like any other. Few restrictions apply to CAP loans. In some states, they may be any size and used for nearly any purpose (U.S. Treasury, 1998).

If the loan is paid off without problems, the initial fees deposited by both the business and the government stay in the fund. In this way, the fund builds up over time. However, if the loan stops performing and goes into default, the bank would begin the normal collections process, attempting to recover any collateral guaranteed as a part of the loan deal. If, after recovery has been fully pursued, the bank still suffers losses because of the loan in question, the bank may charge those losses against the CAP loan loss reserve fund, drawing it down.

What Are the Advantages to the Community?

The advantage to the state or local community is a larger number and array of successful small businesses. Research confirms that banks are induced to increase the risk spectrum they will consider and will loan more to small businesses because of the improved protection. Primarily benefited are businesses that have minor collateral problems (Hamlin, 1998).

Because the program is set up to rely on market forces to "police" many of the details of loan deals, government spends very little time or money on the program. Research indicates that governmental expenditures per job created can be less than $300 (Hamlin, 1999), and easily recovered through added tax revenues. Participating loans also seem to have a low failure rate. Nationally, over the fourteen years the program has existed, and after approximately one billion dollars worth of total loans have been made, only 3.9 percent or about $39 million worth of loans have gone into default. A much smaller percentage have needed to tap into reserve pools since many loan losses are covered by collateral recovery. As a result, CAP reserve funds now contain about $50,000,000, or more than 4.9 percent of cumulative CAP loan volume (U.S. Treasury, 1998).

In those states in which a program already exists, the local economic development planner can play a communication role. He or she may work with nonparticipating local banks to promote their involvement and may inform businesses having trouble obtaining conventional financing about the program and the banks that use it. Since CAP loans have few restrictions, they can be included as a part of a larger financial package that could include local revolving loan funds, certified development company loans (SBA 504), or other seed capital (Michigan Jobs Commission, 1996). The local economic development director or incubator manager can help put together these packages.

A study of the Michigan program, the nation's largest, indicates that few businesses or local economic development offices know about the program, and few bank loan officers know how CAP can work with other sources of financing. The state makes little effort to inform people of CAP's existence except through the banking community (Hamlin, 1998). Plenty of work remains for local economic development coordinators to enhance the value of the program for their community. Where no CAP program exists, local development professionals should work to establish one, either at the state or local level.

Where Is It Used?

CAP programs are found in twenty states and two municipalities (U.S. Treasury, 1998). The U.S. government is considering national legislation that would provide incentives for the remainder of states to participate and would support existing programs with modest contributions to local reserve funds (Jones, 1998). The concept is being considered in other nations (Hamlin, 1999). Conceivably, any governmental jurisdiction could establish a program. All CAP requires is (1) a legal structure, (2) willing and capable lending institutions, and (3) enough governmental contribution to the loan insurance pools to share some of the risk and keep the required business fees within a range such that businesses are willing and able to participate.

Social Capital Building for Business Retention

What Is It?

An emerging strategy for local and regional economic development is social capital building. Interest in this approach was sparked by discussions of social capital building in the industrial regions of Italy by Robert Putnam and others. While some have pointed out that the political culture in Italy is quite different from that in the United States, that has not stopped some in this country from documenting and experimenting with social capital building, American-style, for economic development. One of the most celebrated examples of this is the transformation of Tupelo, Mississippi, from a poor rural community to a dynamic, economically strong city that boasts an enviable quality of life. This was accomplished largely through the development of a set of intricate social and economic networks over a thirty-year period (Grisham, 1999).

The concept of "social capital" is not a new one, but it has received renewed attention over the past decade. It is, at its essence, the networks that exist among people. Coleman (1988) has described it as being a fourth form of capital, along with financial, human and physical capital, that is an input to productive activity; however, he also views it as an input to the development of human capital, itself. Social capital consists of linkages within the organization (internal linkages) and linkages between that organization and other individuals and organizations outside of it (external linkages). Social capital may be formal in nature, as in the creation of institutions to perpetuate certain linkages, or informal (e.g., a loose confederation of groups that comes together to accomplish a certain mutually held goal). Its success depends on trust among the individuals and groups involved, norms that are

mutually respected, channels for mobilizing information and other resources, and the willingness and ability of network members to accept
a diversity of perspectives (Coleman, 1988; Flora and Sharp, 1997; Servon, 1997). It also requires a facilitative champion.

In the realm of local economic development, social capital building is
generally a strategy for linking local businesses to encourage economically beneficial activities, linking economic development service providers to make them more efficient and effective, or both. As an
example, Lichtenstein and Lyons (1999) have created a system for de-
termining the skill levels of entrepreneurs, assigning those of similar
levels of skill to a group, and providing strategically targeted skill-
building assistance to that group that permits its member firms to
advance to the next higher skill level. This system also organizes enterprise development service providers (e.g., business incubators, microenterprise programs, Small Business Development Centers, etc.) to
provide service at the entrepreneurial skill level(s) most appropriate to
their expertise, eliminating service overlap and identifying service
gaps. This system is designed to operate much like the professional
baseball league system and is called the Entrepreneurial Development
System. Among its many tools, this system utilizes extensive social
capital building among client entrepreneurs, service providers, mentors, and other parties to ensure that a true transformation of client
businesses and the local economy takes place. This system underlies
the case that will be described below wherein social capital building is
used to retain manufacturing businesses in neighborhoods of inner city
Philadelphia.

What Is Its Purpose?

In general, the purpose of social capital building in economic development is to create a social and economic infrastructure that will support economic growth. This is accomplished by building networks
between and among businesses and economic development assistance
providers that permit the smoother flow of information and resources
that facilitate economic activity and growth.

A related purpose for building social capital in the economic development arena is to create the environment for transformation. Whether
explicitly stated or not, the chief goal of all economic development activity is to transform the local or regional economy from its current
state to one of optimal vitality. This is very difficult, if not impossible,
to do one business at a time through arms-length transactional rela-

tionships among businesses and service providers. Yet this latter approach is the way in which much economic development activity is undertaken (Lichtenstein and Lyons, 1999). Through social capital building, nurturing relationships that can spawn actual transformations are developed and sustained over time.

How Does It Work?

Economic development-related social capital building efforts, while similar in many respects, vary according to their purpose. The effort offered as an example in this section is aimed at retaining and revitalizing manufacturing businesses in the inner city as a community development strategy. It is known as the Urban Industrial Initiative (UII) and was established as a three-year pilot program by the Philadelphia Industrial Development Corporation (PIDC) in collaboration with the Pew Charitable Trusts. PIDC is a partnership of the City of Philadelphia and the Greater Philadelphia Chamber of Commerce. The targeted neighborhoods constitute a 10-square-mile portion of lower Northeast Philadelphia and are home to more than 330 manufacturing businesses from a wide variety of industry sectors (Lichtenstein, 1999). These firms employ approximately 13,000 workers, and are crucial to the economy of central Philadelphia (Lichtenstein, 1999).

As Lichtenstein (1999) reports in his description of UII, its goal was to retain jobs by assisting these inner city manufacturing firms in a way that was useful to them and complementary to the efforts of numerous other entities in the community that had business retention as their mission. In order to do this in the most effective way possible, PIDC held personal interviews with the operators of over 100 of the manufacturers in the target neighborhoods. The results of these interviews led them to some important conclusions that shaped UII's approach. Chief among these were: (1) the demand for technical assistance to firms cannot merely be assumed; it must be created by helping firms to understand what their true needs are, and (2) the development of technical skills alone is not the key to growing successful businesses; developing entrepreneurial and managerial skills is more valuable (Lichtenstein, 1999, p. 7).

PIDC was aware that they, and the other business assistance service providers in the area, had only limited resources. They were also cognizant of the fact that the UII must strive to better link the manufacturing firms to their neighborhoods if they hoped to retain the businesses once the latter had become economically stronger. Thus,

PIDC knew they needed a strategy that would leverage additional resources and make it economically attractive for their target firms to stay in their neighborhoods.

The resultant strategy was one of social capital building as defined by networking the manufacturing companies with each other to pool resources, share expenses, engage in buy from/sell to relationships, exchange information, and form strategic alliances. It was believed that this strategy would help the manufacturers build skills, grow their firms, and develop relationships that would make it economically viable, even expedient, to physically stay put. It was also expected that through facilitating this social capital building process, PIDC would develop relationships with these firms that would permit a better understanding of their needs and how best to connect them with appropriate and useful assistance (Lichtenstein, 1999).

The implementation approach used by the UII in carrying out this strategy included a number of key elements. First, UII began with those firms it called "spark plugs." These were firms that were either leading edge, had the most potential for high economic impact, or already had extensive linkages to other businesses in the community. It then used one-on-one meetings with these firms' operators to both build trust and diagnose each firm's needs. Diagnosis of need is one of the key features that makes the UII approach truly innovative. Third, the UII instituted ways to maintain ongoing contact with each firm: contact that goes beyond assistance referrals to the kind of support that renders transformation.

Smart Park

What Is It?

A smart park is an industrial/office park that focuses on high technology businesses and contains many features not found in traditional business parks, including a high level of electronic connectivity, laboratory research, and advanced meeting facilities, to name a few.

What Is Its Purpose?

In addition to providing high-quality space for high-tech firms, the purpose of the smart park is to facilitate the transference of pure research findings and inventions into marketable products and services. Technology transfer is a complex process, and the park's purpose is often more related to facilitating communication than it is to providing space. The local community's purpose in promoting a smart park may be to diversify and upgrade its economic base. In most cases, the successful smart park can increase the average income of a community by attracting higher skilled outside businesses and residents into the area.

Who Operates a Smart Park?

Any private entity can form and operate a smart park, although they are often set up by a government or with government subsidy as a means of stimulating and transforming a local economy. Nonprofit organizations and universities have also been park developers. Because of the mixed land use, the multifaceted purpose already mentioned, and other complexities, some governmental or quasigovernmental partnership is nearly always present.

How Does It Work?

One of the purposes of including this section in this book is to emphasize how much is required to create a successful smart park. This is not an endeavor that any community should take lightly. A large number of efforts across the country will undoubtedly fail, and the competition will be great. Success seems to come from the synergy of many factors and the absence of one or more of these factors may greatly reduce the chance of success.

A smart park can be organized physically as a traditional industrial park. It can be a large area divided into parcels that are sold or leased to appropriate companies. (Successful smart parks have been from 150 acres to thousands of acres.) It should be located with convenient access to both air and ground transportation. To turn this traditional physical structure into a successful smart park requires, at a minimum, several special characteristics. Some of these are as follows:

- A common vision for the park:

  Common vision means a clear understanding and a consistent message by the community, the developer and the occupants about the park's purpose, industrial emphasis, style of operation, community relationship, business image, and worldwide marketing strategy for both the park and its occupants.

- Advanced meeting facilities:

  The purpose of the smart park is as much the facilitation of communication as it is the provision of space. The park must start with the most basic form of communication, face-to-face, and integrate it with the most advanced digital information technology. The meeting facility must therefore be completely multimedia equipped and must provide space for both small intensive meetings and theater presentations in a luxurious environment. The meeting center should be at the center of the park, but with easy access to the outside world and fast access to an airport facility.

• Lodging:

To facilitate the kind of communication that must take place at a smart park, the highest quality lodging facility must be present, located next to the meeting center.

• Relationships with nearby universities:

The park can be adjacent to a university or a few miles away. This relationship can involve joint research, the sharing of scientists' time, the involvement of a university fund or foundation in the establishment of pre-venture capital, the use of common laboratory facilities, and the sharing of the university's reputation through proximity, to name a few.

• A high-tech incubation facility in the park:

As with any incubator, the purpose is to provide a common point for small business development through the education and training of new entrepreneurs while minimizing start-up difficulties. The facility would include small efficient spaces and use of common facilities and services. However, as a part of the technology transfer process, the high-tech incubator is less concerned with providing low-cost space and more concerned with linking new technologists with venture capitalists and appropriate markets. Yet, high-tech entrepreneurs often need the basics of business management, including training in taxation, finance, managerial accounting, personnel, intellectual property law, and community relations (Lichtenstein and Lyons, 1996).

• Nonprofit research institutes located in the park:

These are often nonprofit organizations set up, owned, and controlled jointly by universities, university foundations, chambers of commerce, and/or local industry. They typically focus on one industry such as microbiology. The institutes' physical facilities can contain advanced laboratories that are shared by the university, the institute, and corporate park occupants. These non-profit institutes often act as intermediaries in the process of technology transfer. A scenario might be for such an institute to use pre-venture capital to purchase product development rights related to a university-generated scientific discovery and carry out further research to invent practical applications. The institute may then spin off products in separate for-profit corporations that seek venture capital. The new corporations may then locate in the park's high-tech incubator until they are large enough to become major park tenants (Herbert, 1999).

- Sources of venture capital and preventure capital with offices located in the park:

In a central core office complex, university foundations, governmental organizations, economic development offices, and private venture capitalists should have offices to facilitate business access to venture and pre-venture capital.

- Digital audio and video internet connections between the meeting facilities, the rooms in the lodging facilities and various park companies, research institutes and nearby universities, for advanced meeting and information sharing; and

- Availability of high-quality, high-speed connectivity with the internet and other networks such as Internet2 and vBNS to all locations in the park and to the outside world:

The Internet2 project is organized by a consortium of more than 170 U.S. research universities known as the University Consortium on Advanced Internet Development (UCAID). It seeks data transfer speeds many times faster than the internet, which makes it ideal for transfer of large amounts of research data, real-time experimentation and simulation, and audio and video transmission. The controlling consortium has endeavored to keep Internet2 focused on research activity, but will have wide business application. Early corporate sponsors of Internet2 included Bell South, Compaq, Ericsson, Novell, Litton, SBC Communications and Storage Tek (University Consortium on Advanced Internet Development, 1999).

- Satellite parks with high-level connectivity to the central park:

These smaller parks may be in smaller communities tens of

miles away but are linked to the core or hub park organizationally and electronically. This strategy takes advantage of the footloose nature of broad-band electronic communication while adding to the critical mass of business expertise that can be tapped by the hub park. For a small community, seeking partners to become a satellite may be a better strategy than going it alone (The Michigan Technology Park Network, 1999).

- High-quality labor force and labor force services:

Engineers and scientists can be attracted to a region if the region has an adequate quality of life, good university connections, and strong growth prospects for the professional's area of technology. With the growing number of two professional breadwinner families, communities that are so small and/or isolated that spouses have trouble finding employment appropriate to their skills will have trouble developing a successful smart park hub. The semiskilled labor force need not have a high level of specialized technical training. It is more important that workers have strong basic skills and employability skills and are trainable. Local universities, community colleges, and skill centers should be very cooperative and flexible in working with businesses to assist with specialized training as needed (Muth et al., 1979).

- An attractive setting:

This includes both the attractiveness of the smart park and the surrounding region. Most high-tech parks have strict planning and landscaping standards and covenants. High-tech companies often take great pride in the physical setting of their corporate facilities.

- Other quality-of-life features including but not limited to the following:

  1. Excellent public schools
  2. Good health care
  3. Adequate quantity and quality of housing, including executive quality housing nearby
  4. Recreational and entertainment opportunities including performing arts, sports, and outdoor activities

In addition to all these smart park features, it also helps if the park is a part of a corridor of high-tech activity. Corridors are regional urban agglomerations that develop along transportation or communication lines or take on a linear form because of geographic constraints. The urban pattern can look like a string of beads rather than an urban belt. Some technology corridors, such as the 128 Corridor, developed as a natural confluence of forces (Rogers and Larson, 1984; Rosegrant and Lampe, 1992; Saxenian, 1994; Gromov, 2000; Mackun, 2000). Others, like the North Carolina Research Triangle and Silicon Valley, were at least partially induced by a set of intentional public or university policies applied to the right confluence of natural forces.

What Are the Advantages to the Community?

The advantages of a successful smart park to the community are numerous. They include the following:

- A rapid growth in employment
- A diversification of the economic and employment base
- An upgrading of the wage and skill level of employment
- Increased demand for cultural activities from upper income professional workers and their families
- Spin-off benefits of a strengthened link between the local university and the local business community
- Stimulation of other development in the region

A negative secondary effect of success might be that higher prevailing wage levels drive out businesses that cannot afford to pay higher wages. Small business development using appropriate technologies might be a better economic development strategy than a smart park for many communities.

Where Is It Used?

Many large universities across the country have promoted a nearby smart park and have participated with local communities to establish them. Some cities have tried to use the high-tech park concept as a form of brownfield or infill development such as in the case of Milwaukee's Triangle Commerce Center.

States have also participated in smart park promotion. As an example, many states have promised to use tobacco settlement money to stimulate biotechnology or life sciences agglomerations including smart parks and research corridors. The State of Michigan has pledged one billion dollars of the tobacco money to fund life sciences research at four anchor universities within a "life sciences corridor" (Burgess, 1999; Singhania, 1999). Part of the money is designated for commercialization of research results through smart park creation, pre-venture capital, and other initiatives. Ohio has announced a similar proposal.

To truly understand the concept, U.S. local economic development professionals need to be receptive to learning from other nations. Japan has developed Tsukuba Science City (Tsukuba Science City, 2000), a 189,000 population satellite new town surrounding a large smart park containing a university, several governmental and private research institutes, corporate laboratories, offices, and production facilities. Korea is working on Kyongso Information New Town, connected with the giant Yongjongdo New International Airport project, to be the transportation and communication hub of the Yellow Sea region (Hamlin, Lyons, and Lee, 1996); a nonprofit foundation is building Capricorn, a technology park with all the attributes for success in the Cape Town, South Africa, urban region (Capricorn, 1999; Mulla, 1999); Malaysia is promoting its Multimedia Super Corridor (Multimedia Super Corridor, 2000); and Singapore, one of the most electronically connected places on earth, is developing its technology corridor (Corey, 1999). At least a hundred other more modest efforts are under way or on drawing boards all over the world. As was recently pointed out, the only place not trying to be Silicon Valley is Silicon Valley.

Procurement Program

What Is It?

A procurement program is a program of educational and technical assistance by the local economic development office to assist local business in selling to federal and state governments.

How Does It Work?

There are two components of a procurement program. One is an educational component and has as its purpose to educate local businesses to the advantages and pitfalls of dealing with large governments. It lets them know what kinds of products and services can be sold to government. It also tells them what procedures to follow and where to make contact. The second component is a program of technical assistance and shared services that directly assists businesses in making the necessary government contacts and following through on them.

What Are the Advantages to the Businesses?

The advantage to local businesses is the opening up of a large market they may not have tapped. The federal marketplace is larger and more diverse than people realize. The U.S. government purchases over $230 billion worth of goods and services a year, and this expands by more than $5 billion annually. Despite the perception that most purchases are of military hardware, Uncle Sam buys a wide variety of items including, for example, $106 million worth of books, maps, and publications, $2 million in musical instruments, phonographs, and home radios, and $60 million in toiletries. Nearly all businesses can find a U.S. government buyer for their product.

Selling to government can offset seasonal and cyclical slumps, making the local business more stable, smoothing the production process, and avoiding layoffs. Government buys consistently. Although the types of items purchased may vary, the magnitude of governmental outlays changes little from year to year.

Federal procurement is very complex, however. Despite efforts at unified purchasing, each agency has a different procedure for handling its procurement, thereby requiring that small businesses receive substantial assistance with improved protocol. Businesses in communities that have a sophisticated procurement program have a great advantage over those in communities that do not.

What Are the Advantages to the Community?

In addition to general economic growth resulting from more successful businesses, a procurement program offers the following advantages:

1. It helps to stabilize the local economy by offering countercyclical outlets for local production.
2. It promotes the success of local businesses rather than relying on attracting new businesses for economic growth.
3. If businesses appreciate the benefits of the service, they are less likely to leave the community.

Where Is It Used?

Communities all over the country have short-term programs designed to provide information about procurement. Procurement seminars are sometimes offered to incubator tenants. Often a congressional office will assist in setting up seminars on federal procurement and invite the entire local business community. The public relations benefits of such a program can be substantial to congress members. Ongoing programs of coordination, shared services, and technical assistance are rare, however.

What Does It Take to Make It Work?

Even the smallest and shortest of programs provides some educational benefit at relatively low cost. Allowing one local business to make one successful contact could have enormous long-term implications for the community. In general, however, a procurement program must provide ongoing technical assistance and support to have a major impact on the community.

Rapid Industrial Preparation Program

A light industrial firm establishing a new location normally has a strong reason for that decision. Whether the new location is a relocation or a new branch facility, its establishment is usually in response to a perceived market trend, competitive pressure, or some other need critical to that business's future. As a result, the business owner often wants to accomplish the move quickly.

Because of this perceived need for haste, the choice of an industrial location is not always well thought through. The selection is often made with limited data and much intuition on the part of top company officials. Although a small industrial concern may have carefully chosen the general region of its new location, the exact site and the particular community may be determined by short-term expediency.

The need for swift action creates frustration for the small business owner since choosing a site and erecting and equipping a building can be a complex and lengthy process. Land must be chosen which is the right size, location, and price; building plans must be prepared; zoning changes and site plans approved; financing arranged; contractors hired; utility hookups made; and loans and sales closed. The result is that the business often locates in the community in which it can start operations the soonest. Communities that offer a quick move have an advantage.

One method available to cities for dealing with this issue is to establish a publicly owned industrial park. In this way a business can purchase a lot with available utilities, with few zoning issues to deal with, and in a good location for regional transportation. However, a city must undertake a great financial risk in making the front-end investment of buying and subdividing land and supplying all utilities for a complete industrial park. Because of an oversupply of industrial space, most communities that have publicly developed industrial parks have had to carry a large financial burden. Furthermore, when a community develops an industrial park, it damages the incentive for private developers to develop industrial space. The result might be less industrial land at higher cost. Municipal industrial parks have not turned out to be a cost-effective economic development tool in most communities. A more cost-effective approach is to implement a "rapid industrial preparation" (RIP) program. An RIP is a mechanism for quickly providing space for businesses interested in locating in the community without the front-end costs or competition with the private sector.

What Is It?

An RIP program consists of two parts. The first part is a semiformal organization of individuals who have key roles in the process of helping a prospective new business acquire and prepare space and begin operations. The second part is a clearly laid out, step-by-step procedure that the various individuals previously mentioned follow from the time a business expresses interest until they are located and operating in the community.

How Does It Work?

The steps are as follows:

1. The local government or other organization cooperating with the Economic Development Committee purchases options on about three parcels of industrial property of varying size and location. The organization purchasing the options could be the community's new venture fund or similar organization. The option should establish a fixed sale price. The option should be transferable, but should give the property owner some control over the kind of business to which the option could be trans-

ferred. The land should have all utilities ready, be properly zoned, and have clear title.

2. A set of plans for a modifiable speculative building are drawn up, including a set of standardized accompanying site plans.

3. A contractor ready, willing, and able to construct the speculative building is identified and a price estimated.

4. Each of the potential legal interactions with the city or other governmental unit is listed (e.g., site plan review, historic commission review, sign ordinance, and so on), and someone serving the function of the economic development coordinator is prepared to walk the prospective business through that process, providing assistance where necessary.

5. A mechanism for providing financing for the plant and equipment is established. The person acting as a finance coordinator is prepared to do a preliminary screening of the project and the business, determine the project's financial feasibility and eligibility for special financial incentive programs, and then carry the proposal to the appropriate financial intermediary.

6. Linkages are established with schools, community colleges, and vocational centers to provide customized training for newly hired local employees of the business. This training takes place before completion of the building so that the business can reach full operation as soon as possible.

Example

In the event that an interested industrial firm is found to be compatible with the community, a person acting as economic development or finance coordinator would meet with the prospective business. He or she would indicate on which parcels of industrial property the community held options to see if any fit the locational and financial criteria of the firm. The owner of the property would be contacted to see if there were any objections to the firm or type of building being contemplated. The coordinator would present the speculative building plans to the business staff and work with them to create a preliminary modified building plan and cost estimate for a building that meets the firm's needs and fits on the selected site. He or she would then describe the legal review process existing in the community, including presenting the text of relevant laws and scheduling meeting dates. The firm would start that process to the extent possible. The coordinator would then do a preliminary financial screening of the business and the project to see if financing is possible and if any special programs are relevant. This set of steps should be completed within a few days of the initial meeting.

At this stage, if everything indicates that the project should proceed, the firm would contract to finalize building plans and site plans and obtain final cost estimates. They would begin the legal review process, contact appropriate financing organizations, and buy the option from the community-based organization at a price that covers the purchase price plus other administrative expenses associated with purchasing and carrying the option. They would also contact training organizations, if specialized training of future employees were helpful, so as to design such training. In this way several necessary steps are proceeding simultaneously with the help of the economic development coordinator.

Once all building plans are completed and legal approvals received, the business would purchase the land and begin construction of the building. On completion of the building, the work force should be trained and industrial operations ready to begin.

Options

The option that the city or community organization purchases gives it the right to buy the land at a specified price at any time during the period of the option. The period is the time from the option purchase date to the expiration date. Both the specified purchase price of the land and the expiration date are matters of negotiation that affect the price of the option contract. An exclusive option not only gives the option buyer the right to buy the land, but takes the land off the market for all other prospective buyers until the expiration date. An exclusive option is much more expensive. Little need for an exclusive option exists in this case since the city's objective is to fix a land price and ensure land availability for a prospective light industrial activity, rather than reserving land for its own development.

Modifiable Speculative Building Plan

A speculative building plan consists of working drawings for a building that can be quickly modified to meet a business's specific needs and then used to erect a building quickly. In other words, the building is a standard design utilizing readily available materials and components.

It is formulated in such a way as to be easily modified with minimal damage to the economics of the standard design. The economic development coordinator should have a set of drawings for the standard building on hand, with knowledge of how to make regular modifications.

How Much Does It Cost?

The cost of purchasing an option on industrial land depends on negotiations between the city and the landowner. It also depends on the fixed price of the land and on the expiration date. The longer the period or life of the option, the greater the extent to which the owner must be compensated for potential inflation loss. An option that expires in three years with a fixed or striking price equal to the current market value of the land will cost between 5 and 10 percent of the price of the land plus projected inflation.

Detailed plans for a speculative building as described above could cost approximately $17,000–$23,000. These plans are then reusable since they act as the basis for all modified plans.

Backshop Development Program

Historically, a backshop was a back room in an obscure part of a building or loft. There the activities of a business were placed that did not require public exposure, so as to utilize low-rent space. As central business districts began to demand very high rents, backshops were moved to lower-rent districts, adjacent to downtown areas. Today, with advanced communication technologies, backshops may be hundreds of miles away from the main office.

What Is It?

A backshop development program is a specific effort on the part of the development office of a community with a low cost of living to induce higher-cost service firms to identify which aspects of their operation could experience cost savings and move them to the lower-cost community. Here, we are not talking only about lower rent, but lower costs in general. The lower-cost community may be another part of the same city or in a different metropolitan area.

What Is Its Purpose?

The purpose of a backshop development program is to develop the economy of the lower-cost community through the promotion of spillovers of employment and wealth from higher-cost regions, while promoting the success of the business located in the higher-cost region through cost savings. The purpose is not to promote the lower-cost region at the expense of the higher-cost region, however. The firm's success will also benefit the region of its home office.

How Does It Work?

Step one of the backshop development program is to contact firms in higher-cost areas and offer free analysis of the firms' operations to see if money could be saved by moving some components of the business to the lower-cost area.

Step two is to provide the analysis to interested firms. The study must be done by experts in operations analysis and job development. Comparisons are made not only for rent savings, but also for savings on other expenses. When located in a labor market different from the main office, one of the biggest savings of the backshop may be wages and fringe benefits.

When a firm agrees to move a part of its operation, step three of the process is to set up the transportation and communication linkages necessary to allow the backshop to function at some distance from the central office. If located in a small, out-of-the-way, low-income community, fast mail delivery can be a problem. If the backshop handles large amounts of mail, a post office box can be established in a large metropolitan area and mail can be trucked to the office. The U.S. Postal Service will do this for high-volume customers.

Computer linkages present another problem. Typically computer information is transferred via the internet as a part of the company's extranet operation. Extranet is internal communication between various geographically separated branches of a firm. Extranet uses the internet backbone to move information from one company office location to another, but with firewalls and other security at each location. For company employees, the extranet behaves like an intranet or internal company network (Edwards 1999; Orfali, Harkey, and Edwards, 1999). To use the system, each location must either have direct Ethrnet or other broadband access to the internet or must call using a telephone modem. Telephone modems are very slow and inappropriate for backshop operations whose primary function is information processing, and if there is no local gate to the network, the call may be long distance.

The fourth step is to set up a targeted training program to ensure that people in the initiating low-cost community can be quickly trained to take over the proposed backshop operation. This means identifying potential employees, ensuring that they have adequate general and basic skills, and solving other employability problems before moving the backshop. It also means setting up an on-the-job training program so that training can begin as the backshop commences operation.

What Are the Advantages to the Business?

A lowered cost of operations constitutes the advantage to the business. Substantial differences exist between labor markets for the cost of low-skill jobs. If located in a low-cost labor market, savings can be as much as 50 percent of the cost of operation for the backshop activity.

What Are the Advantages to the Community?

In addition to general economic development and job-creation for the lower-cost community, several additional benefits are apparent. First, backshop operations tend to be labor-intensive and employ a broad spectrum of individuals. In high-unemployment areas they may employ large numbers of low-skill workers. Second, they employ a broad spectrum of space. Because of the service nature of the backshop operations, and the lack of need for public exposure, they can locate almost anywhere in the community. Third, a backshop development program, even when it operates in the same labor market as the front office, can bring jobs closer to handicapped and transportation-disadvantaged people. A fourth advantage of a backshop development program is that it usually offers a clean form of economic activity because backshops tend to be office or paper service activities. Fifth, just the process of setting up the program helps to establish contacts with successful firms in other areas that might lead to greater economic ties and exportation of goods and services in the future.

Where Is It Used?

Many private firms look for backshop savings as a part of good business practice, and the financial services industry has evidenced interest in the concept. Large numbers of Manhattan firms have established backshops in Brooklyn in recent years, partly as a result of public sector efforts.

Insurance companies offer a good example of the use of backshops, although they do not like to call it a backshop. Inside the processing unit, they establish external offices. One must be careful not to call these regional or branch offices since they do not serve a specific region of the country. Rather, they are organizationally a part of the head office, but located in lower-cost communities. These external offices process premium checks sent by policyholders or other routine tasks.

Elmira, New York, a declining community in the northern part of the Appalachian region, had high unemployment for almost fifteen years, resulting from numerous plant closings. However, Elmira had a well-educated workforce eager for employment.

About seventeen years ago Aetna decided to set up a check processing center in New York State because of the large amount of business exposure. Company managers saw this effort as a way of cutting costs as well. Elmira was chosen because of the quality of the labor force. Aetna took over 8,000 square feet of Eastern Mall, a small enclosed mall suffering from low occupancy built near the CBD. Owned by the city, the mall was constructed as a part of a major building program following a severe flood in 1972. The high-quality space rented for $12 per square foot in 1988, as compared with $35 per square foot in Hartford. Employees have indoor parking attached to the mall.

In Elmira, several special efforts were made to ensure good transportation and communication from this somewhat out-of-the-way city to the home office and the rest of the world. A post office box with a Buffalo zip code was established, for example, and 50,000 pieces of mail per day were trucked from it to the Elmira office, and telephone companies installed special lines.

About 98 percent of the 208 first employees in Elmira were locals hired as a result of the move. Semiskilled people were paid 10 cents over minimum wage, plus piecework bonuses. Training was set up prior to moving the backshop. Elmira employees have been productive, and turnover and absenteeism have been low.

Although few want to claim substantial wage savings resulting from the Elmira backshop, local employees face a much lower cost of living than they would in the headquarters city. A house of comparable size and amenities may cost 50 percent less in Elmira.

The operation was so successful as a cost-cutting effort that a second location was established in Elmira by taking over an attractive old post office building in the CBD and completing a renovation of it. More recently, as a part of corporate restructuring, the entire operation was sold to Travelers Insurance Group. In 1998 the city worked with Travelers to renew their lease on the mall space. Travelers wanted to combine its Elmira operations and take over the entire mall to house 300 employees. To accommodate Travelers, Southern Tier Economic Growth (STEG), the local economic development agency, worked with

New York's Empire State Development Corporation to provide new loans and training grants to Travelers. The city refurbished or built 160 parking spaces and included the mall in its enterprise zone (Johnson, 2000). Elmira has now used the backshop strategy for over seventeen years to fill downtown space and provide hundreds of high-quality jobs to local residents (Iraci, 2000).

What Does It Take to Make It Work?

The first prerequisite of a successful backshop development program, run by an economic development office, is marketing focused on high-cost business areas. The commitment to seek out prospective firms must exist before considering the establishment of a program.

The most important component, however, is expertise in job analysis and development. What the lower-cost community really sells to the firm in the higher-cost district is expertise in making its business operate more efficiently. Establishing a reputation and credibility is an important part of the marketing effort. For a variety of reasons, operating the program as a consortium of businesspeople, rather than a government agency or authority, is usually beneficial.

A third component of a successful program is an emphasis on training. Ensuring that people are trained to take over the backshop in its new location is a stickier problem than normally perceived and takes an intensive effort. It is key to a smooth transition.

A successful program must be sensitive to the politics and economics of both affected communities. An unexpected concern is the need for sensitivity to the pride of the low-cost community. Although the low-cost community appreciates the increase in employment resulting from a backshop program, they sometimes resent the negative connotation of backshop. The low-cost community does not want to feel taken advantage of because it is being paid lower wages than other employees of the same company for the same work. In general, people need to feel that being a low-cost community comes from success at maintaining a competitive edge, not from economic failure that puts them at a disadvantage. The successful backshop development program works to capitalize on that competitive edge for the benefit of the business and both regions. It also works to assure employers in the lower-cost communities of their essential role in the effort.

Foreign Trade Zone

What Is It?

U.S. foreign trade zones are places located inside the United States, but legally outside U.S. Customs territory. In these zones, goods from foreign countries can be stored, exhibited, processed, fabricated, and reshipped abroad, without payment of customs duties. A foreign trade zone is not a free port like St. Thomas, Virgin Islands, or the local cigarette store at the international airport, and it is not a bonded warehouse. The functions of a bonded warehouse are similar, but it provides only storage.

What Is Its Purpose?

Historically, and from the perspective of the U.S. Customs Service, the purpose of a foreign trade zone has been to promote foreign trade and help U.S.-based firms compete in international markets. It does this by reducing the burden of tariffs for firms that use foreign inputs and/or ship their product overseas. Historically, nearly all zones were found near major port facilities such as New York and San Francisco. Now, small and medium-sized communities in all parts of the country see the program as a tool for economic development.

Who Operates a Foreign Trade Zone?

A local nonprofit corporation, such as a port authority or an economic development corporation, applies for and operates a foreign trade zone. The application is relatively easy if the potential operation can demonstrate enough tenant demand to finance the zone, including Customs agent costs. The Trade Zone Commission approves applications for trade zone status. A for-profit corporation interested in being included in a zone must work with a local economic development organization to pursue an application.

How Does It Work?

Generally, foreign trade zones set up for economic development purposes are small industrial parks and warehouse facilities located near a customs port of entry. Most of the facilities are owned by the trade zone operator and rented to interested businesses. The operator provides a common warehouse facility for the businesses in the park. Some land and facilities in the zone can be privately owned. The trade zone operator sets rent on facilities it owns in conjunction with the U.S. Customs Service. The operator and the U.S. Customs Service jointly administer the zone, with the operator primarily acting as landlord and the U.S. Customs Service regulating the transfer of goods in and out of the zone.

The above describes the operation of a general purpose zone, but subzones can also be created. They are separate manufacturing facilities outside the boundaries of a general purpose foreign trade zone. They can either be attached to a general purpose zone or be independent. A subzone attached to the trade zone in Granite City, Illinois, for example, consists of a single automobile plant and is located across the state border in Missouri.

Any item eligible to be brought into U.S. Customs territory can be brought into a foreign trade zone. In addition, items not allowed to enter the United States because of import quotas may often enter foreign trade zones. For example, if the United States puts quotas on the number of Taiwanese VCRs that can be imported into the country, VCRs in excess of the quota can go to foreign trade zones. Later, if quotas are lifted, they can then pass into U.S. customs territory. In the meantime, they may be altered to meet U.S. electrical standards, using U.S. labor.

What Are the Advantages to the Business Community?

Advantages to the business community of being located in a trade zone are:

1. Customs duty and internal revenue taxes are paid only when a firm transfers merchandise from a foreign trade zone to U.S. customs territory for domestic consumption.

2. Goods may be exported from a zone free of duty or taxes.

3. Customs procedures at trade zones are streamlined.

4. The U.S. Customs service provides security at the site to protect against theft and vandalism.

5. Merchandise may remain in a zone indefinitely.

6. If a manufacturer imports parts or raw materials to a plant in a zone, and then sells finished products to the U.S. public, he or she can choose whether to pay tariff on the raw materials or the finished product, thus saving tariff costs.

Businesses not located in the zone but in the same community may benefit from an increased market if they sell goods and services to firms located in the zone.

What Are the Advantages to the General Community?

In addition to job-creation and economic development promoted by the zone, a foreign trade zone can add a new dimension to the local economy. If it succeeds in attracting foreign firms or domestic companies that export heavily, the community generates leads and contacts with other international firms. Since foreign business cycles are often out of phase with U.S. business cycles, firms that export heavily will help to balance cyclical trends and broaden the economic base.

Where Is It Used?

Most trade zones are still located in large port cities. Some of the other communities that now have zones include Dorchester, South Carolina; Shenandoah, Pennsylvania; Sault Ste. Marie, Michigan; Granite City, Illinois; Battle Creek, Michigan; Campbell County, Kentucky; Burlington, Vermont; and Lincoln, Nebraska. Battle Creek is one example of a small community that established its zone primarily for local economic development purposes and, with some marketing assistance from the state, has been successful in attracting new businesses.

What Does It Take to Make It Work?

Many communities feel that if they could become a foreign trade zone, they would automatically attract foreign firms. In reality, it is easy to become a zone, but not easy to attract business to it. It takes large foreign marketing efforts, including travel to trade fairs in foreign countries. This creates excessive costs for a small city, unless it receives support from its state government. Zones do not generate much employment themselves, and the firms that locate there are often not labor-intensive. A zone has a greater chance of succeeding if a community already has a situation that could benefit from trade zone status, such as a local firm that imports raw materials and then exports much of its finished product.

5

Program Evaluation

After having devised an economic development program, its evaluation is important. Evaluation provides the only means whereby the success of the action plan can be assessed and adjustments, if necessary, can be made. This evaluation takes place at several stages. First, programs should be evaluated before implementation. In other words, the plan should be tested. Second, an ongoing evaluation should be carried out during implementation. This essentially involves continuing to collect key pieces of information that allow one to measure a program's progress toward intermediate-level objectives, as described in Chapter 1. Third, the entire action plan should be evaluated after implementation or at the end of specified review periods, such as the end of one year. In each case, the results of evaluation should be fed back to previous steps in the process for review and revision.

Because economic development programs are short range, action-oriented, and people-oriented, an evaluation method that relates to each phase of evaluation and involves those who participate in economic development will offer greater continuity and accuracy. The second section of this chapter concentrates on evaluation prior to implementation, essentially a process of program selection and prioritization. The discussion leads to a method of periodic economic program evaluation which carries through the entire process. First, however, a statement on evaluation and quantification is necessary.

EVALUATION AND QUANTIFICATION

Program evaluation is typically the weakest component of the planning process. One reason for this weakness is that the process of evaluation seems so complex. Anyone who shies away from quantitative analysis is immediately intimidated by evaluation methods. Therefore, some may not evaluate at all. Program evaluation is muddled in extremism. The prevailing attitude is that either you have a Ph.D. in it, or you do not do it. This situation is truly unfortunate. To put the issue in perspective, remember the following:

1. Program evaluation makes judgments about what mix of projects and activities to undertake—nothing more.
2. Program evaluation is and should be primarily a subjective, intuitive, opinionated process.
3. No matter how quantitatively sophisticated the evaluation technique, it builds on a subjective foundation. All evaluation methods are full of assumptions and arbitrary decisions.
4. The objectives on which evaluation criteria are based are subjective inputs.

We live in an era in which we belittle intuition as lazy and unintellectual. In reality, the human brain's complexity far surpasses what any mathematical model can simulate. When we use intuition, we are reaching into our own hidden computational powers in ways that no quantitative technique allows. In fact, becoming bogged down in an excessively sophisticated evaluation model will cloud our intuitive powers and do more harm than good. In decision-making, the purpose of an appropriate level of quantification is to discipline intuition, not replace it.

PRE-IMPLEMENTATION EVALUATION

Prior to carrying out the economic development program, the economic developer should undertake a final review of it to see that the program spends money correctly. Some form of benefit-cost analysis is typically suggested as an evaluation technique to assist in the selection of a mix of projects. A review by business and community leaders offers one of the best methods for pre-implementation evaluation of the economic development program. The following section briefly discusses the application of benefit-cost analysis to economic development programs. It then describes the cross-impact matrix method of analysis, which it suggests as a good mechanism for combining quantitative analysis, subjective analysis, comments by community leaders, and group discussion into a method of cost-effectiveness analysis.

Benefit-Cost

One way to determine the priority of projects or economic development programs is benefit-cost analysis. Actually, benefit-cost refers to a family of evaluation methods with various ways of measuring benefits and costs. These are variously called cost-efficiency analysis, revenue-cost analysis, cost-effective analysis, and complete benefit-cost analysis. In each case a ratio is calculated to determine benefits per dollar of cost. The projects with the highest ratio are listed as the highest priority.

Cost-efficiency analysis is primarily a private-sector tool used in industries that produce a clearly defined homogeneous product through repetitive processes. The cost-efficiency ratio is the cost per unit of production. This measure has little applicability to public sector economic development programs.

Revenue-cost analysis relates costs to a clear, albeit narrow, public-sector objective: the raising of public revenues. The ratio depicts the project or program expenditures required to raise a dollar of public revenues.

Cost-effectiveness analysis has greater public-sector program applicability and attempts to define public-sector accomplishments broadly. Here, production or effectiveness is the accomplishment of predefined goals, and a high ratio implies a high level of goal attainment per dollar spent. However, the ratio compares abstracts to dollars. It is not a dollar-to-dollar ratio.

Benefit-cost analysis attempts to accomplish the same thing as cost-effectiveness analysis, but produces a dollar-to-dollar ratio by translating the full spectrum of benefits to the community of any project or program into dollar quantities. This ambitious undertaking implies an understanding of the secondary impacts of any action and places a dollar value on a wide range of abstracts that are difficult to monetize. For benefit-cost analysis and the other methods mentioned above, all monetary quantities related to future benefits and costs are discounted to

Figure 5.1
Simplified Benefit-Cost Example

The community of Anytown is seeking to develop its stagnant economy. The town council is considering an economic development strategy that includes the establishment of a small business incubator, a one-stop shopping small business development center, and a backshop development program. The overall program will cost $100,000/yr. over the first four years. Beginning in the second year, it will yield benefits for two years of $50,000/yr., and $150,000/yr. in Years 4, 5, and 6. Should the town council consider adopting this program, using a market rate of 11% as the discount rate.

Total Benefit = $50,000 (1.8116) + $50,000 (1.7312) + $150,000 (0.6587) + $150,000 (0.5935) + $150,000 (0.5346) = $345,160
[the numbers in parentheses represent the present worth factors at 11% interest and can be found in any set of compound interest tables]

Total Cost = $100,000 (0.9009) + $100,000 (0.8116) + $100,000 (0.7312) + $100,000 (0.6587)
            = $310,240

Net Benefit = Total Benefit - Total Cost

       = $345,160 - $310,240

       = $34,920

Benefit-Cost Ratio = Total Benefit/Total Cost

              = $345,160/$310,240
              = 1.11

Because net benefit is positive and the benefit-cost ratio exceeds 1, in this case, the town council may want to further explore this program; however, because the values of these two indicators are relatively weak, modifications to the program may be in order.

present value, commonly using the market rate of interest (see Figure 5.1).

Literature on benefit-cost analysis abounds, so no further discussion is needed here except to state one caution. Despite their appearance of rigor, all of the above mentioned methods are highly subjective. Subjectivity emerges in three areas: (1) the monetization of abstract costs and benefits; (2) the implication of cause and effect in secondary benefits; and (3) the selection of a discount rate or public-sector internal rate of return. Although the first two are self-explanatory, the third is more subtle. The discount rate discounts future costs and benefits to their present value. If one values quick paybacks or returns that more than monetarily equal returns coming in a more distant future, then one chooses a high discount rate. If long-range benefits are sought, a lower rate is acceptable. While private-sector firms have some guide as to a desired internal rate of return, rate selection in the public sector is more arbitrary. But a slight change in discount rates can have large impacts on the evaluation of multiyear projects.

Cross-Impact Matrix

Given the previous statements made about quantification and participation, a program evaluation method is sought that guides and disciplines thinking without muddling it, and which involves the principal implementers of the plan. A cross-impact matrix method can accomplish this.

Figure 5.2 shows a simple cross-impact matrix. In the first column, all the projects or activities that make up the economic development program are listed. At the top of each of the next several columns are annual measurable objectives of the economic development program. Intermediate-range measurable objectives might also be listed. These objectives cover a set time period, typically one year. A grid remains that cross-references projects with objectives. Some programs are set up such that each activity has a one-to-one correspondence with each objective. Although fairly simplistic, nothing is inherently wrong with this approach. It may be more imaginative to design a project that helps to attain several of the objectives originally set forth. Even in a program with a one-to-one correspondence, secondary effects and unintentional spillovers often exist.

The next step is to go through the list of projects, and assign a score for each cell of the matrix. That is, assign a score for each project corresponding to each objective. The score will be from 1 to 100, with 100 the best score. The score in the first cell means "the percentage of the attainment of objective A that would be contributed to by successful completion of project 1." In Figure 5.3, for example, the number 45 indicates that if project 1 were carried out, it would contribute to the attainment of 45 percent of objective A.

The scores placed in each cell can be derived in a variety of ways. One way is to "guesstimate." A second is for a group of people who understand the proposed program to make their own estimates and

Figure 5.2
Cross-Impact Matrix

					totals
GOALS → ACTIVITIES ▶					
TOTALS					

Figure 5.3
Cross-Impact Matrix: Projects' Contributions to the Attainment of Objective

GOALS ▲ ACTIVITIES ▶	A. Employ 80% of those currently unemployed			totals
#1	45			45
#2				
#3				
#4				
TOTALS	45			45

compare them. The group could be the entire staff, the planning commission, the private industry council, a group of businesspeople, and so on. The estimates provided by the various members of the group could be combined in a kind of Delphi technique. Numbers can be averaged through a discussion to work out a consensus. Other more elaborate methods may also be used to arrive at the number in each cell, including simulation techniques.

After establishing a value for each cell, the next step is to add the columns and enter a total at the bottom (see Figure 5.4). What happens if the sum of any column adds up to more than 100 percent? In some cases, this may not be inconsistent. If the established quantitative goal was to create 100 jobs, it may not be undesirable to create 110 jobs, for example. If this turns out to be the case, perhaps the objective was not as difficult to attain as originally thought. One might go back and make the original objective more ambitious. One might also decide that because of limited resources, projects should be reduced in size. The matrix helps in deciding which projects to reduce (see Figure 5.5).

In some cases, depending on how the objective was written, it may be impossible or illogical to attain more than 100 percent of an objective. In this case, one must rethink the true impact of each project on each objective to see if original estimates were too optimistic. It may also be that projects duplicate in their impact, and that in combination with other projects, any given project will not be as effective as originally thought. This overlap may be a sign of waste that should be eliminated. This entire process promotes a group discussion that helps members of the advisory board think clearly about the ramifications of each project.

After each of the cells of the matrix is revised such that the columns add up to 100, add the rows to obtain a total for each project. When reading the rows, one should not think of the numbers as percentages, but rather as points. Points need not add up to 100. In fact, the point total for each project represents a score for that project (see Figure 5.6).

A cross-impact matrix can be made more sophisticated in a variety of ways. However, because its true value lies in its simplicity and ease of understanding, one must remember that each increase in complexity may cause a reduction in ease of use. One procedure that is useful in making the matrix more accurate, for example, is to rate objectives. It may be that some objectives are more important than others. If this is true, objectives can be weighted. A rating of the importance of the objective (say, from 1 to 10) might be written at the top of each column.

Figure 5.4
Cross-Impact Matrix: Summing Impacts

GOALS ▲ ACTIVITIES ►	A. Employ 80% of those currently unemployed	B. Increase tax base by 30% for industrial property		totals
#1	45			45
#2	33			33
#3				
#4	33			33
TOTALS	111			

Figure 5.5
Cross-Impact Matrix: Reconciliation of Impacts

GOALS ➤ ACTIVITIES ➤	A. Employ 80% of those currently unemployed			totals
#1	45			45
#2	33			33
#3				
#4	22			22
TOTALS	100			

Figure 5.6
Completed Cross-Impact Matrix

GOALS ➤ ACTIVITIES ➤	A Employ 80% of those currently unemployed	B. Increase tax base by 30% for industrial property	C. Increase employment in countercyclical industries by 20%	totals
#1 Management assistance program for firms with less than 20 employees.	45	5	20	70
#2 Business retention survey and follow-up program	33	20	5	58
#3 community media and trade show program	0	25	0	25
#4 targeted revolving loan fund	22	20	20	62
TOTALS	100	70	45	

153

Then when rows are added to obtain the score for each potential project, the score in each cell is multiplied by the rating, or weight, listed at the top of its column. The totals in the far right-hand column then become weighted totals reflecting the objectives' varying importance. All of this can be avoided by constructing a set of measurable objectives in the beginning that are roughly equal in importance.

The cross-impact matrix system provides the beginning step in a cost-effectiveness evaluation system. The score in the far right column measures the effectiveness of the project. Dividing this score by the dollar cost of the project or program produces an effectiveness/cost ratio. Projects should then be prioritized according to which exhibits the highest ratio. If the matrix represents a twelve-month plan of targets and programs, then cost figures can be used at face value. If, however, the matrix depicts several years, cost figures must be discounted to net present value before being used in the ratio.

ONGOING AND POST-PROGRAM EVALUATION AND FEEDBACK

A secret to success in any endeavor is the ability to monitor one's progress toward objectives. This is important not only to estimate progress, but also to continuously reassess one's targets and directions. In a complex project or program, this requires an organized system of ongoing evaluation. The key ingredients of an ongoing evaluation system are: (1) setting meaningful and measurable objectives, as described in Chapter 1; and (2) establishing an information system that provides a continuous flow of monitoring information concerning the impact of programs and the achievement of objectives, as described in Chapter 2. Ongoing evaluation and feedback therefore involves maintaining information systems and using information to determine the extent to which projects are contributing to the achievement of objectives.

New information concerning the results of projects and programs, and monitoring the change in a community's economic situation, should feed back to impact the entire planning process. There are several reasons for this. First, new knowledge may cause objectives to be redefined. Second, if measurable objectives change, this may lead to new data needs to monitor progress toward new objectives. Third, new knowledge may cause a reassessment of the impact of projects on the attainment of objectives. In other words, even though the project or program is being successfully implemented, control group evaluation techniques or other methods may conclude that cause and effect relationships between the action and the desired ends are not what was originally estimated. Furthermore, experience with a project or program may cause one to reestimate total costs.

One advantage of the cross-impact matrix as a cost-effectiveness evaluation system is that it can be used to test a plan prior to implementation, and can then be maintained throughout implementation. All of the changes mentioned above, resulting from the feedback of new information, can be incorporated into the cross-impact matrix. New or altered measurable objectives are listed across the top. The numbers representing the impacts of projects on objectives can be changed to produce new effectiveness scores. Finally, reestimated costs can then be applied to these scores to obtain new cost-effectiveness ratios. This process offers a continuous reprioritization of projects.

Measurable objectives should be written to measure achievement on an annual basis (or some other predetermined period that is consistent across all projects). Therefore, once each year a more intensive "post-implementation" evaluation should be conducted, using both objective evaluation techniques and group discussion. The result of this step is a new set of objectives, a new or revised set of actions or projects, and a revised management information system.

CONCLUSION

Program evaluation is what makes the planning process interactive and dynamic. It permits the plan to be reviewed and refreshed, ensuring its utility over time. This is especially crucial in the world of economic development planning, which changes almost daily.

Because program evaluation by its very nature is subjective and qualitative, an economic development specialist should not shun it, fearing a lack of the necessary expertise. It is basically a simple activity in which all practitioners should engage. The procedures described in this chapter are designed to make program evaluation a do-able, useful, nonthreatening activity that will enhance the quality of any given economic development action plan.

6

Summary and Conclusions

SUMMARY

Economic development continues to be an important and widely recognized activity of local government. Cities and states are increasingly more flexible in their attitudes toward the role of government in economic development. Governmental and quasi-governmental organizations are aggressively promoting their local economies in ways not considered appropriate in the past. This is particularly true with respect to the forms of collaboration between the public, private, and nonprofit sectors that have evolved. In fact, the boundary between public and private has blurred as governments have become more entrepreneurial and businesses have increasingly recognized the value of factoring the public interest into their activities. "Third sector" organizations, which lie between pure public and pure private, continue to flourish. This has served to increase the complexity of local economic development.

In response to this growing intricacy, training and educational opportunities for practitioners have proliferated. Despite this, economic development activities continue to be narrowly focused on job-creation, and in too many places an inordinate amount of attention continues to be paid to attracting businesses to the community. Economic development must become a part of a more carefully considered planning process in all communities. This does not mean that it should be undertaken by technocrats or be purely long-range and theoretical. It must be real and action-oriented; it must embody the economic desires of a broad spectrum of the community's citizenry.

An important preliminary step for a community is to clearly understand in its collective mind why it should plan for economic development. This comprehension must be in both practical and theoretical terms. In practical terms, if a community does not consciously and continuously work to protect and expand its local economy, it may become vulnerable. Its economic base may quickly erode through the exertion of national and global economic forces. In an electronic world, billions of dollars of wealth can flow from one location to another in a matter of seconds, based on decisions made by people in a very distant place. Preserving local wealth can no longer be left to chance.

In theoretical terms, economic development planning implies some sort of formal or informal intervention by government in the economy. One must therefore know what it means to intervene in a predominately market-oriented economy. Markets respond quickly to new economic forces, creating secondary and tertiary reactions throughout the system. The best-intended community actions can create effects that are the opposite of those desired. It is the opinion of the authors that the best economic development action plans work, in most cases, to perfect market mechanisms rather than block their functioning.

The planning process is a continuum that carries the community from the normative step of delineating values and setting goals to the more specific and objective stages of carrying out, or implementing, action. Evaluation takes place at every stage, and the results of any given step loop back to redefine earlier steps. The steps of the action planning process can be defined as:

1. Set goals and establish measurable objectives.
2. Gather needed information and build knowledge.
3. Create an annual plan consisting of a set of actions to attain measurable objectives.
4. Implement planned actions.
5. Evaluate and feed back information for the next cycle.

The first step should involve extensive community discussion probing the most encompassing community values, but should end with a specific limited set of measurable objectives. The objectives of economic development should not merely be to create jobs or attract businesses. A vast array of other objectives might also be considered, including retaining existing employment, enhancing the municipal tax base, increasing property values, retaining wealth within the community (or, in the current parlance, making the community more economically sustainable), reducing poverty, and stabilizing the economy. Establishing measurable objectives means that annual targets are stated in such a way that not only can their achievement be discerned, but progress toward their attainment can be measured.

Collecting information and building knowledge needed to make decisions is the second step. Data collection is time-consuming and expensive. Decisions are always made with incomplete data, and the planner must continually balance the cost of information with the benefits of improved actions. Knowledge is built by developing theories. Theories are tested using time-series information and comparing results with anticipated consequences. Historic trends and the product of the evaluation step are important sources of knowledge.

Successful economic development planning requires that the public sector planner understands the businessperson's point of view. One way for the planner to adopt and maintain a business manager's perspective is to organize information according to the questions that a typical business needs answered, based on its requirements. To operate successfully, nearly every business needs all of the following:

1. Land

2. A labor supply

3. Physical capital

4. An energy supply

5. Financing

6. Management skills, including marketing information and know-how

7. Favorable tax rates and equitable tax treatment

8. Resources to carry on effective product and market research

9. A community with a good quality of life for its employees and consumers

The most important data elements for economic development planning are those necessary to measure progress toward measurable objectives.

Step three is formalizing an action plan, which consists of a limited set of specific actions to be completed in a defined period. Action statements should delineate actions to be taken in the next year. They should be specific, precise, and clearly designated. Actors should be individuals or organizations over whom the local government has some control, or private individuals who have expressed a willingness to carry out the planned action. Action statements should state clearly the location of the action and, where necessary, detail the steps required for completion of the action. Secondary effects of the action should also be anticipated and expressed. Implementing the planned action over the course of the year is step four of the process. Step five is evaluation of progress. In fact, evaluation takes place continuously throughout the process and provides feedback knowledge to previous steps.

CONCLUDING THOUGHTS

Increasing collaboration between the public, private, and nonprofit sectors continues to be one of the most important trends in economic development ten years after the publication of the first edition of this book. Innovative thinkers in all three sectors have created mechanisms for promoting the accomplishment of public policy and meeting the needs of the community while at the same time compensating investors and entrepreneurs for risking their personal and financial capital. These intersectoral partnerships span the full range of economic development activities, from small-scale, bottom-up efforts such as microenterprise or empowerment business incubation programs to massive, top-down urban redevelopment projects and multistate regional manufacturing networks. This process has continued to make government more inventive and to foster a sense of enlightened self-interest on the part of the business community.

This trend has been with us now for nearly forty years, going back to the urban renewal authorities of the 1960s that were arguably important pilots for the partnership strategy. The Urban Development Action Grant (UDAG) program of the 1970s was another significant antecedent to today's brand of public-private partnership. In the 1980s, the worst economic recession since the Great Depression and the Reagan administration's version of "New Federalism" made it very clear that neither private business nor state and local government could develop economies alone. While abuses of these partnerships still occur and skepticism among some persists, years of trial-and-error experience continue to prove that innovative liaisons between public, private, and nonprofit organizations can be, and are, accomplished without perversion, and that the goals of all of these organizations can be achieved. The very fact that intersectoral partnerships have persisted this long suggests that a paradigm shift in economic development may have occurred. One thing is certain: This strategy has not succumbed to the faddishness that has plagued so many other economic development approaches as they fall in and out of political favor (Dewar, 1998).

Several societal forces, which were emerging in the 1980s and early 1990s, have continued to gain strength and have sustained the public-private partnership phenomenon. They are:

1. Planners and policy makers are placing amplified faith in the use of market mechanisms to accomplish public policy.

2. The nonprofit sector has grown substantially and plays an increasingly important role in the U.S. economy.

3. Citizens have become ever more aware of the results of businesses abusing their privilege and taking advantage of imperfect markets. It is troubling to note that the nature of most of these abuses has not changed substantially in the past ten years. A few visible examples are:

   a. Environmental calamities such as oil spills, the illegal burying or dumping of hazardous waste, and the aftermath of earthquakes that reveal shoddy construction practice;

   b. Sudden plant closings affecting an entire community;

   c. Continued central city physical and social deterioration, and the resultant isolation of a permanent underclass;

   d. Various stock market investment scandals.

4. Most businesses, however, have realized the long-term consequences to them of poor citizenship and the resultant effects listed in item 2.

5. Most businesses have become more experienced and more comfortable working with governments for mutual benefit.

These ongoing trends continue to have the significant implications for the theory and practice of local economic development planning that they had a decade ago. The trends offer insight regarding future career paths for students and future research agendas for academicians as well. The implications are worldwide in scope.

On the one hand, these trends imply that both researchers and practitioners must continue to strive to have a better understanding of market mechanisms, how they work, when they work, and when they do not. Many opportunities to accomplish considerable public good have been lost and many public dollars have been misspent as a result of inadequate understanding. At the same time, we must not fall into the trap of equating a free-market economy with a laissez-faire economy. We must understand that an unregulated, imperfect market has the potential to cause more damage than no market at all. The cities of the Industrial Revolution of the nineteenth and early twentieth centuries offer ample evidence of this.

We must learn more about the most appropriate way to intervene in markets for the promotion of public policy. This means having both a practical and a theoretical understanding of feedback effects and secondary impacts. This also implies being able to continue to formulate public policy in ways that are new and innovative. Over the past decade we have continued to shift from a public policy definition strictly in terms of government carrying out policy through direct action to one that involves partnerships with the private sector. We must continue to experiment with public, private, and nonprofit interrelationships, looking for ways to more effectively create wealth and build assets throughout our communities.

These ongoing trends also have implications for the ways in which we use information. Availability and access to data is no longer a problem. Growth in the number and size of data bases in recent years has been phenomenal. The Worldwide Web has made access to this data easy. The challenge lies in making all that information useful to both public and private users. Data's usefulness hinges on the following: (1) ease of use; (2) relational versus hierarchical access; (3) the user's ability to ask the right questions and, therefore, seek the right information; (4) the user's aptitude for choosing and carrying out the right analysis with the raw data; (5) the capacity to display the results in a useful way; and (6) protection of proprietary information (Hamlin and Lyons, 1996). We must continue to explore systems that address all these considerations in a meaningful and affordable way.

The continuing trend toward public-private partnerships has significant implications for democracy, whether referring to local government in the United States, Eastern Europe, or a less developed country. Voters attempt to simplify issues in order to make choices between candidates. For an incumbent this often means taking responsibility for a successful project or program with which voters can easily identify, understand, and link to the incumbent's name. Incumbents therefore have a natural urge to keep control over programs. Carrying out public policy by intervening in markets and establishing formal linkages with private organizations diminishes both control and identification.

Finally, economic development that utilizes complex relationships between government and private companies challenges the moral and ethical fiber of both the legal and cultural system. A greater level of trust is required, and new forms of oversight must be continually created and tested. Ongoing experimentation with mixed systems illustrates that while ethical problems do arise, the challenge can also have the effect of strengthening professional ethics. These programs open up each sector to the scrutiny of the other and induce the actors, and the public at large, to think about and discuss related ethical issues.

Bibliography

Ahlbrandt, Roger S., Jr., and Clyde Weaver. 1987. Public-Private Institutions and Advanced Technology Development in Southwestern Pennsylvania. *Journal of the American Planning Association* 53 no. 4:449–458.

Albert, Burt. 1999. USA Group Acknowledges It Almost Left. *Indianapolis Star*, November 17, A1.

Allen, David N., and Syedur Rahman. 1985. Small Business Incubators: A Positive Environment for Entrepreneurship. *Journal of Small Business Management* 23, no. 3:12–22.

Alliant Energy. 2000. www.alliantenergy.com (March 15).

American Planning Association. 1976. Ask Plan Landers. *Planning* 42, no. 4:31.

Ammer, Christine, and Dean S. Ammer. 1984. *Dictionary of Business and Economics*. New York: Free Press.

Baldwin, John H. 1985. *Environmental Planning and Management*. Boulder, CO: Westview Press.

Bamberger, Rita J., and David W. Parham. 1984. Leveraging Amenity Infrastructure: Indianapolis's Economic Development Strategy. *Urban Land* 43, no. 11:12–18.

Barker, Michael, ed. 1984. *Rebuilding America's Infrastructure: An Agenda for the 1980s*. Durham, NC: Duke University Press.

Barnekov, Timothy, Robin Boyle, and Daniel Rich. 1989. *Privatism and*

Urban Policy in Britain and the United States. Oxford: Oxford University Press.

Berger, Allen N., and Gregory F. Udel. 1995. Relationship Lending and Lines of Credit in Small Firm Finance. *Journal of Business* 68: 351–382.

Berger, Allen N., and Gregory F. Udel. 1998. The Economics of Small Business Finance: The Roles of Private Equity and Debt Markets in the Financial Growth Cycle. *Journal of Banking and Finance* 22:613–673.

Bertsch, Dale F. 1984. Non-Profit Institutions and Urban Revitalization. In Paul R. Porter and David C. Sweet, eds., *Rebuilding America's Cities: Roads to Recovery*. New Brunswick, NJ: Center for Urban Policy Research.

Birch, David. 1981. Generating New Jobs: Are Government Incentives Effective? *CUED Commentary* 3, no. 3:3–6.

Black, Henry Campbell. 1968. *Black's Law Dictionary*. St. Paul, MN: West Publishing.

Blackford, Mansel G. 1991. Small Business in America: A Historiographic View. *Business History Review* 65:1–26.

Blakely, Edward J. 1994. *Planning Local Economic Development: Theory and Practice*. 2nd ed. Thousand Oaks, CA: Sage Publications.

Browning, William D., and L. Hunter Lovins. 1989. *Energy Casebook*. Old Snowmass, CO: Rocky Mountain Institute.

Buccino, Gerald P. 1989. Business Failures Increasing. *Secured Lender* 45, no. 2:24, 26.

Buchanan, Michael R. 1983. *Real Estate Finance*. Washington, D.C.: American Bankers Association.

Burges, Jordan, Matt Corrion, Goh Wee Keng, Justin Linkner, Julie Zutkis, and Roger Hamlin. 1999. The Michigan Life Sciences Corridor. Unpublished working paper. Michigan State University.

Burrus, Daniel. 1993. *Technotrends: How to Use Technology to Go Beyond Your Competition*. New York: HarperCollins.

Campbell, Candace. 1988. *Change Agents in the New Economy: Business Incubators and Economic Development*. Minneapolis, MN: Hubert H. Humphrey Institute of Public Affairs.

Carlson, Cynthia J., and Robert J. Duffy. 1985. Cincinnati Takes Stock of Its Vacant Land. *Planning* 51, no. 11:22–26.

Choate, Pat, and Susan Walter. 1981. *America in Ruins: Beyond the Public Works Pork Barrel*. Washington, D.C.: Council of State Planning Agencies.

Choe, Sang-Chuel. 1993. Asian-Pacific Urban System: Towards the 21st Century-Evolving Urban System in North-East Asia. In Gill-Chin Lim and Man-Hyung Lee, eds., *Dynamic Transformation of Societies*. Seoul: Nanam Publishing House.

Clarke, James W., Julia A. Wyckoff, and Roger E. Hamlin. 1979. *Hydropower Redevelopment: A Manual Emphasizing Utilization of Employment and Training Resources*. East Lansing, MI: Proaction Institute.

Coleman, James S. 1988. Social Capital in the Creation of Human Capital. *American Journal of Sociology* 94 (Suppl. S95–S120).

Conway, H. McKinley, Jr. 1966. *Area Development Organizations*. Atlanta, GA: Conway Research.

Cook, James. 1987. Priming the Urban Pump. *Forbes* 139, no. 6:62–64.

Cooper, Arnold C. Y. The Entrepreneurship-Small Business Interface. In Calvin A. Kent, Donald L. Sexton, and Karl H. Vesper, eds., *Encyclopedia of Entrepreneurship*. Englewood Cliffs, NJ: Prentice-Hall.

Corey, Kenneth E. 1997. Creating and Controlling Cyber Communities in Southeast Asia and the United States. Paper prepared for presentation at the Pacific Rim Council on Urban Development 9th Annual Conference, Westin Stamford, Singapore, October 27.

Corey, Kenneth E. 1999. Intelligent Corridors: Outcomes of Electronic Space Policies. In *E-Space V: 1999 Digital Development: Assessing the Promise of Information Technology*, conference proceedings of the fifth e-space conference in Cape Town, South Africa, July 10–15.

Corey, Kenneth E., Roger E. Hamlin, and Thomas S. Lyons. 1989. Non-Financial Incentives for Real Estate Development in the United States. In *Public-Private Partnerships: An Opportunity for Urban Communities*. Tokyo: Housing and Urban Development Corporation of Japan and Urban Matrix Research.

Corey, Kenneth E., and Patrick K. Kernan. 1993. Local Autonomy and Regional Development: Comparative Analyses and Information-Age Strategies for Korea. Presentation at the International Symposium on Local Autonomy and National Development in Korea, sponsored by the Korean Research Institute for Local Administration, Seoul, October 8.

Dajani, Jarir S. 1978. Infrastructure Design and Impact Assessment: Bridging the Gap. In J. Eugene Grigsby III and Madelyn Glickfeld, eds., *A Symposium on Social Impact Assessment and Hu-*

man Services Planning. Palo Alto, CA: Stanford University Press.

Daroca, Andrea. 1990. Building the Economic Development Team. In Susan G. Robinson, ed., *Financing Growth: Who Benefits? Who Pays? And How Much?* Chicago: Government Finance Officers Association.

Detroit Free Press. 1985. We have a Love-Hate Relationship with Jobs. August 12, 4D.

Dewar, Margaret E. 1998. Why State and Local Economic Development Programs Cause So Little Economic Development. *Economic Development Quarterly* 12, no. 1:68–87.

Donohoe, John P. 1988. Lollipop Condos, Air Rights, and Development Rights. *Real Estate Finance Journal* 4, no. 1:64–68.

Durbin, Steve. 1992. Bluegrass State Poll. *Louisville Courier-Journal*, April 27.

Durr, Marlese, Thomas S. Lyons, and Katherine K. Cornwell. 1998. Social Cost and Enterprise Development within African American Communities. *National Journal of Sociology* 12, no. 1:57–77.

Edwards, Jeri. 1999. *3-tier Client /Server at Work*. New York: John Wiley and Sons.

Farrel, Larry. 1986. Building Entrepreneurship: Global Perspective. *Training* 23 (November 7): 42–50.

Flick, Frederick. 1987. Real Estate Finance Blazes New Trails. *Real Estate Today* 20:22–26.

Flora, Jan L., Jeff Sharp, Bonnie L. Newlon, and Cornelia Flora. 1997. Entrepreneurial Social Infrastructure and Locally Initiated Economic Development in the Metropolitan United States. *Sociological Quarterly* 38, no. 4:623–644.

Fosler, R. Scott, and Renee A. Berger. 1982. *Public-Private Partnership in American Cities: Seven Case Studies*. Lexington, MA: Lexington Books.

Friedman, Robert, and Puchka Sahay. 1996. Six Steps Forward for Microenterprise Development in the United States. *Entrepreneurial Economy Review*, 32–37.

Gilderbloom, John I., Reginald Bruce, Betsy Jacobus, Maurice Jones, Mariann Kurtz, John Markham, Dan McAdams, Rob Mullins, Gloria Murray, Russ Sims, Jack Trawick, Sam Watkins, Jr., and Steve Zimmer. 1994. *How University/Community Partnerships Can Rebuild Lives and Neighborhoods, Annual Report on*

H.A.N.D.S. Louisville, KY: Center for Urban and Economic Research, University of Louisville.

Gilderbloom, John I., and Mark T. Wright. 1993. Empowerment Strategies for Low-Income African American Neighborhoods. *Harvard Journal of African American Public Policy* 2:77–95.

Gilmore, Donald R. 1960. *Developing the "Little Economies."* New York: Committee for Economic Development.

Gladwell, Malcomb. 1996. The Tipping Point. *The New Yorker*, June 3.

Grisham, Vaughn L., Jr. 1999. *Tupelo: The Evolution of a Community.* Dayton, OH: Kettering Foundation Press.

Gromov, Gregory R. 2000. A Few Quotes from Silicon Valley History. http://www.internetvalley.com/svhistory.html (January 18).

Gunyou, John. 1990. Managing Economic Development Resources. In Susan G. Robinson, ed., *Financing Growth: Who Benefits? Who Pays? And How Much?* Chicago: Government Finance Officers Association.

Hagiwara, Schun. 1991. The Fourth Sector in New Planning. Presentation to the 1991 Annual Convention of the Japanese Planning Association, Tokyo, November 12.

Hagiwara, Schun. 1993. Is Now the Time of Growth Management for an Ever-Growing City?: A Case Study of the Tokyo Bay Waterfront Subcenter Project. In Gill-Chin Lim and Man-Hyung Lee, eds., *Dynamic Transformation of Societies.* Seoul: Nanam Publishing House.

Hamlin, Roger E. 1994. The Korean West Coast Development Strategy in the Pacific Rim Era. In *Proceedings of the International Seminar on the Korean West Coast Development.* Seoul: Korean Planners Association.

Hamlin, Roger E. 1998. *The Capital Access Program: An Evaluation of Economic Benefit.* Lansing: Michigan Jobs Commission.

Hamlin, Roger E. 1999. Agency Change: Infusing an Asset Orientation into Your Work. Presented at the National Conference entitled Getting from Asset to Outcomes: Youth Family and Community Development. East Lansing, Michigan, September 9.

Hamlin, Roger E. 1999. *Capital Access Programs Spur Growth.* Urban Policy Briefing No. 99–2. Program in Politics and Policy, Michigan State University.

Hamlin, Roger E., and Florin Sabastian Duma. 1999. The Capital Access Program: Its Application for Eastern Europe. In Ladislau

Gyemant, ed., *European Traditions and Experiences*. Cluj-Napoca: European Studies Foundation Publishing House.

Hamlin, Roger E., and Thomas S. Lyons. 1989. Public-Private Partnerships for the Promotion of Real Estate Development: A Comparison of Selected Practices in the United States and Japan. In Jack Friedman, ed., *Proceedings of the 1989 Annual Conference in San Diego, CA*. Chicago: Real Estate Educators Association.

Hamlin, Roger E., and Thomas S. Lyons. 1990. Public-Private Partnerships for Urban, Regional and Economic Development. Unpublished paper presented to the Pacific Regional Science Conference Organization Summer Institute for Economic Development in the Southeast Asian Pacific Rim. Bandung Institute of Technology, Bandung, Indonesia, July.

Hamlin, Roger E., and Thomas S. Lyons. 1993. Public, Private, and Nonprofit Sector Interactions for Economic Development in a Restructuring World: Implications for Professional Planning, In Gill-Chin Lim and Man-Hyung Lee, eds., *Dynamic Transformation of Societies*. Seoul: Nanam Publishing House.

Hamlin, Roger E., and Thomas S. Lyons. 1996. *Economy without Walls: Managing Local Development in a Restructuring World*. New York: Praeger.

Hamlin, Roger E., Thomas S. Lyons, and Jack H. Knott. 1990. A Policy Information and Planning Model for Urban Redevelopment Through Public-Private Partnerships. Unpublished paper presented to ELF Foundation Essay Competition.

Hamlin, Roger E., Thomas S. Lyons, and J. Lee. Kyongso, South Korea: 1996. New Town at the Heart of East Asian Ecumenopolis. *Economic Development Abroad* 10, no. 5:1–8.

Hamlin, Roger E., and Gail Oranchek. 1987. *Corporate Apartments*. Tokyo: Tokyo Land Corporation.

Hancock, Diana, and James A. Weston. 1998. The Credit Crunch and the Availability of Credit to Small Business. *Journal of Banking and Finance* 22, no. 6–8: 983–1014.

Hegedus, Jozsef, and Ivan Tosics. 1993. Hungarian Housing in Transition. In Gill-Chin Lim and Man-Hyung Lee, eds., *Dynamic Transformation of Societies*. Seoul: Nanam Publishing House.

Herbert, James L. 1999. President and CEO of Neogen Corporation and Member of the Board of Directors of the Microbiology Institute. Interview by Roger Hamlin, November 29.

Holland, Robert C. 1984. The New Era in Public-Private Partnerships.

In Paul R. Porter and David C. Sweet, eds., *Rebuilding America's Cities: Roads to Recovery*. New Brunswick, NJ: Center for Urban Policy Research.

Holtzman, Samuel. 1989. *Intelligent Decision Systems*. Reading, MA: Addison-Wesley.

Horgan, Sean. 1999. Conseco Fieldhouse. How Was It Paid For? *Indianapolis Star*, November 5.

Huddleston, Jack R. 1981. Variations in Development Subsidies under Tax Increment Financing. *Land Economics* 57, no. 3:373–384.

Hula, Richard. 1999. *An Assessment of Brownfield Redevelopment Policies: The Michigan Experience*. PricewaterhouseCoopers Endowment for the Business of Government, Arlington, VA, November.

Hula, Richard. 1999. *New Ways to Redevelop Brownfields*. Urban Policy Briefings 99–1. Program in Urban Politics and Policy, Michigan State University.

Hula, Richard. 1999. *Public Backs Brownfield Redevelopment*. Urban Policy Briefing 99–3. Program in Urban Politics and Policy, Michigan State University.

Huxhold, William E. 1991. *An Introduction to Urban Geographic Information Systems*. New York: Oxford University Press.

Iraci, Samuel F., Jr. 2000. City Manager, Elmira, NY. Interview by Roger Hamlin, August 1.

Johnson, James C. 2000. Economic Zone Coordinator, Southern Tier Economic Growth. Interview by Roger Hamlin, August 2.

Jones, Benjamin. 1998. Special Assistant to the Secretary of the U.S. Treasury. Interview by Roger Hamlin, December 15.

Jones, Oliver, and Leo Grebler. 1961. *The Secondary Mortgage Market: Its Purpose, Performance, and Potential*. Los Angeles: Real Estate Research Program, UCLA.

Juergensmeyer, Julian C. 1985. *Funding Infrastructure: Paying the Costs of Growth through Impact Fees and Other Land Regulation Charges*. Gainesville: University of Florida Press.

Keith, Joanne G., and Daniel F. Perkins 1996. *Thirteen Thousand Adolescents Speak: A Profile of Michigan Youth*. East Lansing: Institute for Children Youth and Family, Michigan State University.

Kim, T. J., L. L. Wiggins, and J. R. Wright. 1990. *Expert Systems: Applications to Urban Planning*. New York: Springer-Verlag.

Kimbal, Ralph C. 1997. Specialization, Risk, and Capital in Banking.

New England Economic Review 24 (November–December): 51–73.

Kretzman, John P., and John L. McKnight. 1993. *Building Communities from the Inside Out: A Path toward Finding and Mobilizing a Community's Assets*. Chicago: ACTA Publications.

Krumholz, Norman. 1984. Recovery: An Alternate View. In Paul R. Porter and David C. Sweet, eds., *Rebuilding America's Cities: Roads to Recovery*. New Brunswick, NJ: Center for Urban Policy Research.

Krumholz, Norman, and John Forester. 1990. *Making Equity Planning Work: Leadership in the Public Sector*. Philadelphia: Temple University Press.

Landis, John D. 1990. Public/Private Development: Techniques of Project Assessment. In Susan G. Robinson, ed., *Financing Growth: Who Benefits? Who Pays? And How Much?* Chicago: Government Finance Officers Association.

Laughlin, James D., and Graham S. Taft. 1995. The New Act of War. *Economic Development Commentary* 19, no. 1:11–16.

Ledebur, Larry C. 1984. The Reagan Revolution and Beyond. In Paul R. Porter and David C. Sweet, eds., *Rebuilding America's Cities: Roads to Recovery*. New Brunswick, NJ: Center for Urban Policy Research.

Levitt, Rachel, ed. 1987. *Cities Reborn*. Washington, D.C.: Urban Land Institute.

Levy, John M. 1981. *Economic Development Programs for Cities, Counties, and Towns*. New York: Praeger.

Levy, John M. 1988. *Contemporary Urban Planning*. Englewood Cliffs, NJ: Prentice-Hall.

Lichtenstein, Gregg A. 1999. Building Social Capital: A New Strategy for Retaining and Revitalizing Inner-City Manufacturers. *Economic Development Commentary* 23, no. 3: 31–38.

Lichtenstein, Gregg A., and Thomas S. Lyons. 1996. *Incubating New Enterprises: A Guide to Successful Practice*. Washington, D.C.: Aspen Institute.

Lichtenstein, Gregg A., and Thomas S. Lyons. 1999. The Entrepreneurial League System: A Revolutionary Approach to Developing Business Talent and Transforming Community Economies. Unpublished working paper. Louisville, KY: Center for Research on Entrepreneurship and Enterprise Development, University of Louisville.

Logan, John, and Harvey Molotch. 1987. *Urban Fortunes: The Political Economy of Place*. Berkeley: University of California Press.

Long, Andre L. 1984. Lecture on State Economic Development Incentives, University of Michigan, September 25.

Lowenstein, Louis K. 1978. The New York State Urban Development Corporation: A Forgotten Failure or a Precursor of the Future? *Journal of the American Institute of Planners* 44, no. 3:261–273.

Lyons, Thomas S. 1987. Making State Incentives Work: The Role of the Local Development Organization in the Economic Development Process. Ph.D. diss., University of Michigan, Ann Arbor.

Lyons, Thomas S. 1990. *Birthing Economic Development: How Effective Are Michigan's Business Incubators?* Athens, OH: National Business Incubation Association.

Lyons, Thomas S., and Roger E. Hamlin. 1991. *Creating an Economic Development Action Plan: A Guide for Development Professionals*. New York: Praeger.

Machemer, Patricia L. 1998. Transferable Development Rights as a Growth Management Technique in Landscape Management: A Case Study Approach. Ph.D. diss., Michigan State University.

Machemer, Patricia L., Michael Kaplowitz, and Thomas Edens. 1999. *Managing Growth and Addressing Urban Sprawl: The Transfer of Development Rights*, Research Report #563. East Lansing: Michigan Agricultural Experiment Station.

Mackun, Paul. 2000. Silicon Valley and Route 128: Two Faces of the American Technopolis. http://www.internetvalley.cpm/archives/mirrors/sv&128.html (January 18).

Mahanty, Aroop K. 1980. *Intermediate Micro-economics with Applications*. New York: Academic Press.

Malecki, Edward J. 1984. High Technology and Local Economic Development. *Journal of the American Planning Association* 50, no. 3: 262–269.

Mann, Ronald J. 1997. The Role of Secured Credit in Small-Business Lending. *Georgetown Law Journal* 86, no. 1 (October): 1–44.

McElyea, R. 1984. Setting Your Sights on R&D Sites. *Industrial Research* 16, no. 5:46–48.

McNulty, Robert H., Dorothy Jacobson, and Leo Penne. 1985. *The Economics of Amenity: Community Futures and Quality of Life: A Policy Guide to Urban Economic Development*. Washington, D.C.: Partners for Livable Places.

Michaels, Patricia. 1997. Energy in America: The Case against Fossil

Fuel. http://environment.about.com/culture/environment/library/weekly/aa081797.htm (August 31) (March 19, 2000).

Michigan Jobs Commission. 1996. Capital Access Program (Informational Report).

Michigan Technology Park Network at Michigan State University. 1999. Unpublished working paper.

Minerbi, Luciano, Peter Kakamura, Kiyoko Nitz, and Jane Yanai. 1986. *Land Readjustment: The Japanese System*. Boston: Oeljeschlager, Gunn and Haia.

Mintzer, Irving M., Alan S. Miller, and Adam Serchuk. 1996. The Environmental Imperative: A Driving Force in the Development and Deployment of Renewable Energy Technologies. Issue Brief No. 1. Renewal Energy Policy Project of the Center for Renewal Energy and Sustainable Technology, Washington, D.C., April.

Mollenkopf, John H. 1983. *The Contested City*. Princeton, NJ: Princeton University Press.

Mulla, Faizel. 1999. CEO of the Capricorn Foundation. Interview by Roger Hamlin, Cape Town, South Africa, July 13.

Mullin, John R., and Jeanne H. Armstrong. 1983. *Westfield Incubator Survey*. Amherst: Center for Economic Development, School of Management, University of Massachusetts.

Multimedia Super Corridor. 2000. http://mdc.com.my/ (January 19).

Muth, C. Robert, and Roger E. Hamlin. 1979. *Preparation for Work in a Changing Economy*. East Lansing: Michigan State University.

Muth, C. Robert, Roger E. Hamlin, and Paul R. Stuhmer. 1979. *Design for the Delivery of Human Resource Services*. East Lansing: Michigan State University.

NASDA. 1986. *Directory of Incentives for Business Investment and Development in the United States*. Washington, D.C.: Urban Institute Press.

NASDA, CUED, and the Urban Institute. 1983. *Directory of Incentives for Business Investment and Development in the United States: A State-by-State Guide*. Washington, D.C.: Urban Institute Press.

NBIA. 1990. *The State of the Business Incubation Industry 1989*. Athens, OH: National Business Incubation Association.

NBIA. 1995. *The 1995 Directory of Incubators and Members*. Athens, OH: National Business Incubation Association.

Nelson, Arthur C., and J. Richard Recht. 1988. Inducing the Residential Land Market to Grow Timber in an Antiquated Rural Subdivision. *Journal of the American Planning Association* 54, no. 4:529–536.

New York, Comptroller of State. 2000. New York's Public Authorities. http://www.osc.state.ny.us/divisions/pubauth/index.htm (March 23).

North Carolina Solar Center. 2000. Databases on State Incentives for Renewable Energy. http://www-solar.mck.ncsu.edu/finance.htm (March 17) (March 26, 2000).

Northrup. 1986. The Land Assemblage and Development Partnership. *Real Estate Review* 16:90–3.

Nystuen, John, D. Frank, D. Zinn, D. Sulistyo, and R. Darmasetiawan. 1991. Computer-Aided Management Advice for Loan Programs Run by Indonesian Village Women. *World Development* 19, no. 12:1753–1766.

Oakey, Ray. 1984. *High Technology Small Firms: Regional Development in Britain and the United States*, New York: St. Martin's Press.

Oliver, Melvin L., and Thomas M. Shapiro. 1997. *Black Wealth / White Wealth: A New Perspective on Racial Inequality*. New York: Routledge.

Orfali, Robert, Dan Harkey, and Jeri Edwards. 1999. *Client / Server Survival Guide*. 3rd ed. New York: John Wiley & Sons.

Osborne, David E., and Ted Gaebler. 1992. *Reinventing Government: How the Entrepreneurial Spirit Is Transforming the Public Sector*. Reading, MA: Addison-Wesley.

Osborne, David E., and P. Plasterik. 1997. Backing the Unbankable. *The Washington Post*, September 14, W07.

Ostrom, Vincent, and Elinor Ostrom. 1971. Public Choice: A Different Approach to the Study of Public Administration. *Public Administration Review* (March/April).

Peek, Joe B., and Eric S. Rosengren. 1998. The Evolution of Bank Lending to Small Business. *New England Economic Review* (March–April): 26–36.

Peterson, Robert A., Gerald Albaum, and George Kozmetsky. 1986. The Public's Definition of Small Business. *Journal of Small Business Management* 24: 63–68.

Pinchot, Gifford. 1986. *Intrapreneuring: Why You Don't Have to Leave the Corporation to Become an Entrepreneur*. New York: Perennial Library.

Porter, Paul R., and David C. Sweet. 1984. Goals, Processes, and Leadership. In Paul R. Porter and David C. Sweet, eds., *Rebuilding America's Cities: Roads to Recovery*. New Brunswick, NJ: Center for Urban Policy Research.

Porter, Paul R., and David C. Sweet, eds. 1984. *Rebuilding America's Cities: Roads to Recovery*. New Brunswick, NJ: Center for Urban Policy Research.

Rafuse, Robert W., Jr. 1991. Financing Local Government. In John N. Petersen and Dennis R. Strachota, eds., *Local Government Finance: Concepts and Practices*. Chicago: Government Finance Officers Association.

Rahman, Aminur. 1999. *Women and Microcredit in Rural Bangladesh: An Anthropological Study of Grameen Bank Lending*. Boulder, CO: Westview Press.

Rayner, Bob. 2000. National Collegiate Athletic Association Unveils Hall of Champions. *Richmond Times-Dispatch*, March 30.

Rice, Mark, and Jana Matthews. 1995. *Growing New Ventures—Creating New Jobs: Principles and Practices of Successful Business Incubation*. Athens, OH: National Business Incubation Association and the Ewing Marion Kauffman Foundation.

Rogers, E. M., and J. K. Larsen. 1984. *Silicon Valley Fever*. New York: Basic Books.

Rosegrant, S., and D. Lampe. 1992. *Route 128*. New York: Basic Books.

Rothwell, Roy, and Walter Zegveld. 1982. *Innovation and the Small and Medium-Sized Firm*. Boston: Kluwer-Nijhoff.

Saxenian, A. L. 1994. *Regional Advantage: Culture and Competition in Silicon Valley and Route 128*. Cambridge, MA: Harvard University Press.

Scheer, Kendall, and Jeff Reynolds. 1999. The Future of Microenterprise Development: What Are the Challenges? *Rural Enterprise Reporter*, September 17, 1.

Schlefer, Jonathan. 1984. Castles in the Air. *Technology Review* 87 no. 5: 74–75.

Schmenner, Roger W. 1982. *Making Business Location Decisions*. Englewood Cliffs, NJ: Prentice-Hall.

Schnidman, Frank. 1988. Land Readjustment. *Urban Land* 47, no. 2: 2–6.

Servon, Lisa J. 1997. Credit and Social Capital: The Community Development Potential of U.S. Microenterprise Programs. *Housing Policy Debate* 9, no. 1: 115–149.

Sharp, Donald E. 1983. State Industrial Finance Authorities: Another

Source of Term Funding. *Journal of Commercial Bank Lending* 65, no. 10:29–35.

Sidor, John. 1982. *State Enterprise Programs*. Washington, D.C.: Council of State Community Affairs Agencies.

Singhania, L. 1999. Tobacco Cash Funds Life Science Alliance. *Detroit Free Press*, July 20.

Site Selection Handbook. 1985. Atlanta, GA: Conway Publications.

Solomon, Steven. 1986. *Small Business USA: The Role of Small Companies in Sparking America's Economic Transformation*. New York: Crown Publishers.

Sorkin, Donna L., Nancy B. Ferris, and James Hudak. 1986. *Strategies for Cities and Counties.: A Strategic Planning Guide*. Washington, D.C.: Public Technology.

Spencer-Hull, Galen. 1986. *A Small Business Agenda: Trends in Global Economy*. New York: University Press of America.

Steiss, Alan W. 1975. *Local Government Finance: Capital Facility Planning and Debt Administration*. Lexington, MA: Lexington Books.

Strahan, Philip E., and James P. Weston. 1998. Small Business Lending and the Changing Structure of the Banking Industry. *Journal of Banking and Finanace* 22, no. 6–8: 821–845.

Sword, Doug. 2000. Lengthy Demolition to Begin on Outmoded Indianapolis Arena in August. *Indianapolis Star*, March 17.

Thomas, June Manning. 1984. Redevelopment and Redistribution. In Paul R. Porter and David C. Sweet, eds., *Rebuilding America's Cities: Roads to Recovery*. New Brunswick, NJ: Center for Urban Policy Research.

Thomsett, Michael C. 1988. *Real Estate Dictionary*. Jefferson, NC: McFarland.

Tornatzky, Louis G., Yolanda Batts, Nancy E. McCrea, Marsha L. Shook, and Louisa M. Quittman. 1995. *The Art and Craft of Technology Business Incubation: Best Practices, Strategies, and Tools from 50 Programs*. Research Triangle Park, NC: Southern Technology Council.

Tsukuba Information Center. 1999. Tsukuba Science City Information. http://www.info-tsukuba.org (October 22).

University Consortium on Advanced Internet Development. 2000. Internet 2. http://www.internet2.edu (January 13).

U.S. Small Business Administration. 1984. *The State of Small Business*. Washington, D.C.: U.S. Government Printing Office.

U.S. Small Business Administration. 1991. *The State of Small Business*. Washington, D.C.: U.S. Government Printing Office.

U.S. Treasury, Department of. 1998. The Capital Access Program: A Summary of Nationwide Performance, Washington, D.C., October.

Vaughn, Roger J. 1984. Rebuilding America: Financing Public Works in the 1980s. In Michael Barker, ed., *Rebuilding America's Infrastructure: An Agenda for the 1980s*. Durham, NC: Duke University Press.

Vaughn, Roger J., Robert Pollard, and Barbara Dyer. 1985. Confusing Job Creation with Economic Development. *The Entrepreneurial Economy* 11, no. 3:2–6.

Weaver, Clyde, and Marcel Dennert. 1987. Economic Development and the Public-Private Partnership. *Journal of the American Planning Association* 53, no. 4:430–437.

Welsh, Robert. 2000. Indianapolis Planning Department. Interview by Roger Hamlin, February 18.

Williams, Kristine. 1986. Business and Industrial Development Corporations (BIDCOs): An Innovative Approach to Small Business Financing. Unpublished paper.

Wolfe, T. 1983. The Tinkerings of Robert Noyce: How the Sun Rose on the Silicon Valley. *Esquire* 100: 346–374.

Woods, Nicole Y. 1999. Children's Festival Reopens Renovated Union Station. *Indianapolis Star*, December 3, D3.

Zorn, C. Kurt. 1991. User Charges and Fees. In John N. Petersen and Dennis R. Strachota, eds., *Local Government Finance: Concepts and Practices*. Chicago: Government Finance Officers Association.

Index

About the Authors

THOMAS S. LYONS is Associate Professor of Management and Urban Policy and Director of the Center for Research on Entrepreneurship and Enterprise Development at the University of Louisville. He is co-author of *Economy Without Walls* (Praeger, 1996).

ROGER E. HAMLIN is Professor and Coordinator of the Urban Planning Program at Michigan State University. He is coauthor of *Economy Without Walls* (Praeger, 1996).